HEROIC ANIMALS
PATRON SNIFFS OUT DANGER
HEROIC BOMB-DETECTING DOG OF UKRAINE

BY **BRUCE BERGLUND**   ILLUSTRATED BY **MARK SIMMONS**

CAPSTONE PRESS
a capstone imprint

Published by Capstone Press, an imprint of Capstone.
1710 Roe Crest Drive, North Mankato, Minnesota 56003
capstonepub.com

Library of Congress Cataloging-in-Publication Data
is available on the Library of Congress website.

ISBN: 9781669057727 (hardcover)
ISBN: 9781669057826 (paperback)
ISBN: 9781669057833 (ebook PDF)

Summary:
During the war in Ukraine, many cities were destroyed, and large areas were left in ruins. Among the rubble were many dangerous, unexploded bombs and mines. But thanks to the hard work of a well-trained dog named Patron, Ukraine's streets have become more secure. Follow along with Patron as he sniffs out hundreds of deadly explosives and helps the people of Ukraine feel safer in their homeland.

Editorial Credits
Editor: Aaron Sautter; Designer: Elyse White; Media Researcher: Rebekah Hubstenberger: Production Specialist: Whitney Schaefer

Image Credits
Alamy: Ukrinform, 29

All internet sites appearing in back matter were available and accurate when this book was sent to press.

Direct quotes appear in **bold, italicized** text on the following pages:

Page 5: "'The Citizens Are Here and We Are Here': Zelenskyy and Team Stand Firm in Kyiv," by NBC News, February 25, 2022, https://www.nbcnews.com/video/president-zelenskyy-posts-defiant-selfie-video-from-ukraine-s-capital-134062661977

Page 20: "Bomb-Sniffing Dogs in Ukraine Discover Mines, Russian Uniforms Left Behind," by Radio Free Europe/Radio Liberty, June 21, 2022, https://www.rferl.org/a/mines-trostyanets-dog-ukaine-russian-uniforms-emergency-service-sapper/31906548.html

Page 23: "Children in Ukraine Master New Mine Safety Skills," by Unicef, August 3, 2022, https://www.unicef.org/ukraine/en/stories/children-in-ukraine-master-mine-safety-skills

Page 27, top left: "Patron the Mine-Sniffing Dog Awarded Medal by President Zelensky," by BBC News, May 9, 2022, https://www.bbc.com/news/world-europe-61376816

Page 27, bottom right: "Zelenskiy Awards Medal to Bomb-Sniffing Dog," by Reuters, May 8, 2022, https://www.youtube.com/watch?v=hZ2pWiNJJ-M

Printed and bound in China.   PO 5593

TABLE OF CONTENTS

Chapter 1: A Small Hero in a Big War 4

Chapter 2: One Clever Dog...............................6

Chapter 3: Guarding Against Danger............10

Chapter 4: Invasion! 14

Chapter 5: Keeping Children Safe 20

Chapter 6: A Most Famous Dog 24

Ukraine's Smallest Hero 29
Glossary 30
Read More 31
Internet Sites.............................31
About the Author.......................32
About the Illustrator 32

Chapter 1: A Small Hero in a Big War

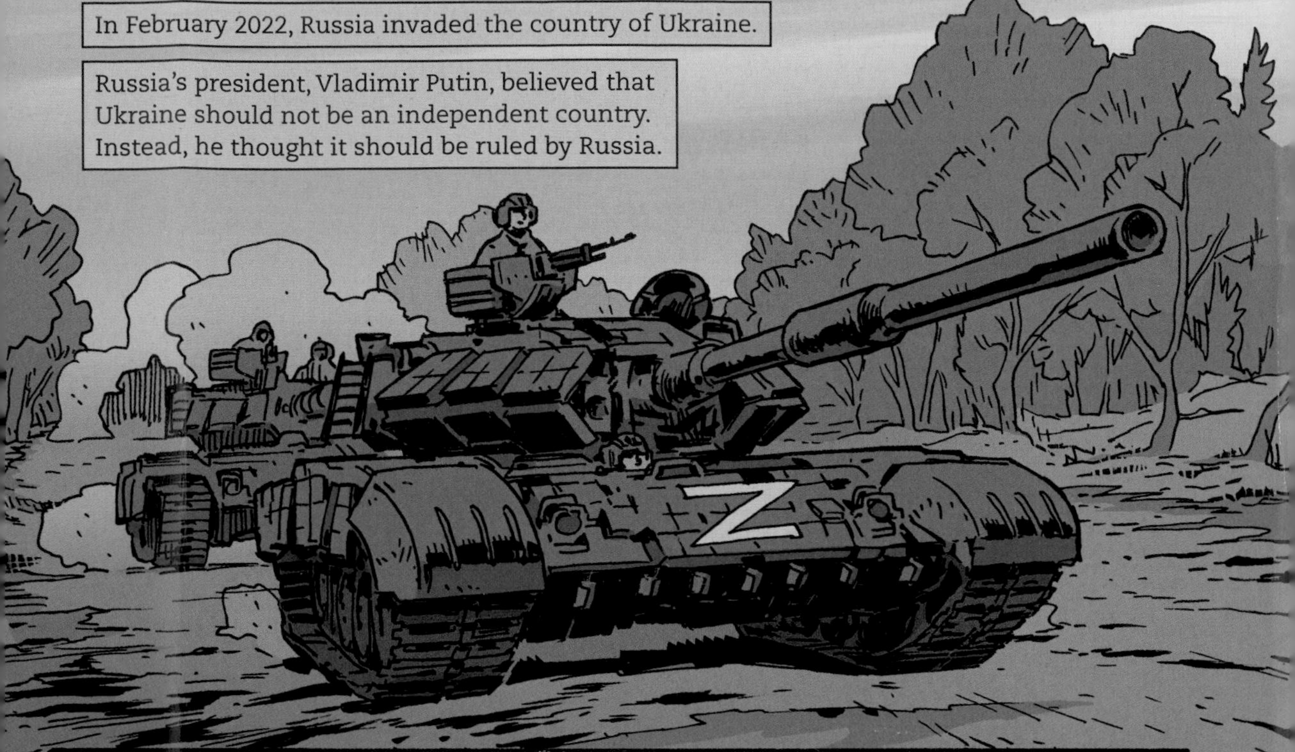

In February 2022, Russia invaded the country of Ukraine.
Russia's president, Vladimir Putin, believed that Ukraine should not be an independent country. Instead, he thought it should be ruled by Russia.

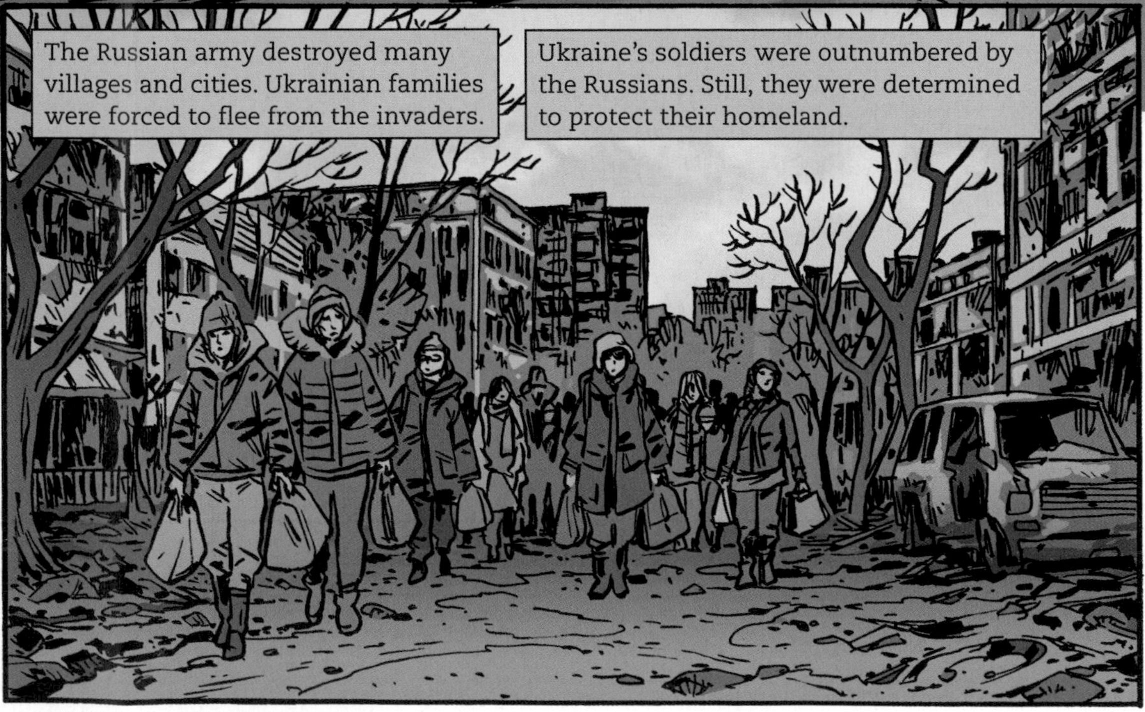

The Russian army destroyed many villages and cities. Ukrainian families were forced to flee from the invaders.
Ukraine's soldiers were outnumbered by the Russians. Still, they were determined to protect their homeland.

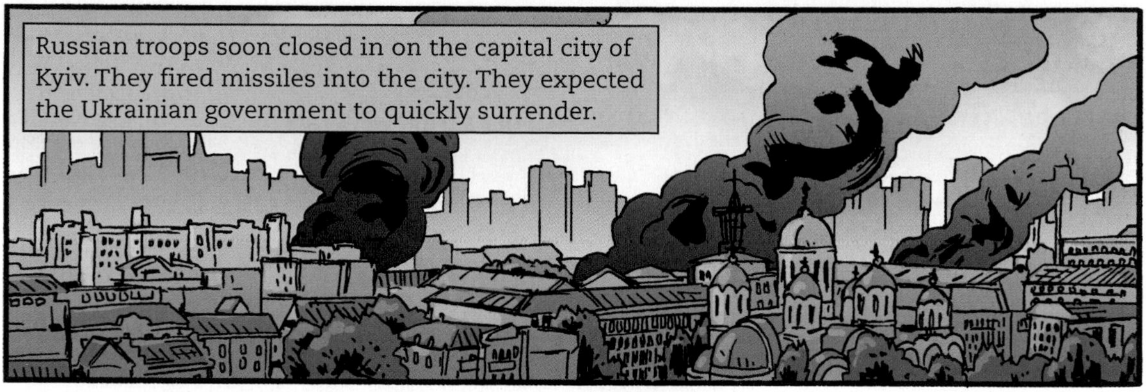
Russian troops soon closed in on the capital city of Kyiv. They fired missiles into the city. They expected the Ukrainian government to quickly surrender.

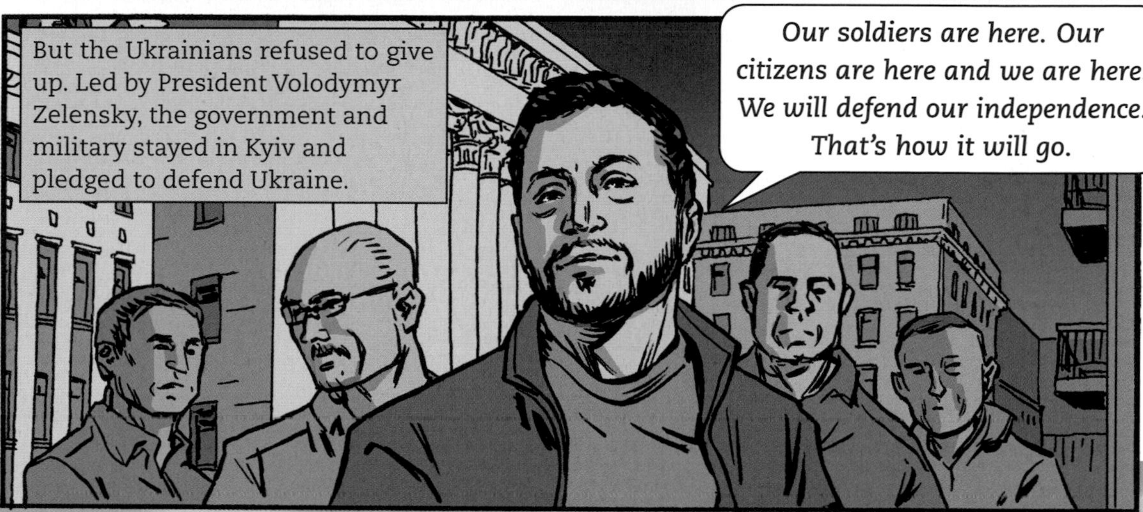
But the Ukrainians refused to give up. Led by President Volodymyr Zelensky, the government and military stayed in Kyiv and pledged to defend Ukraine.
Our soldiers are here. Our citizens are here and we are here. We will defend our independence. That's how it will go.

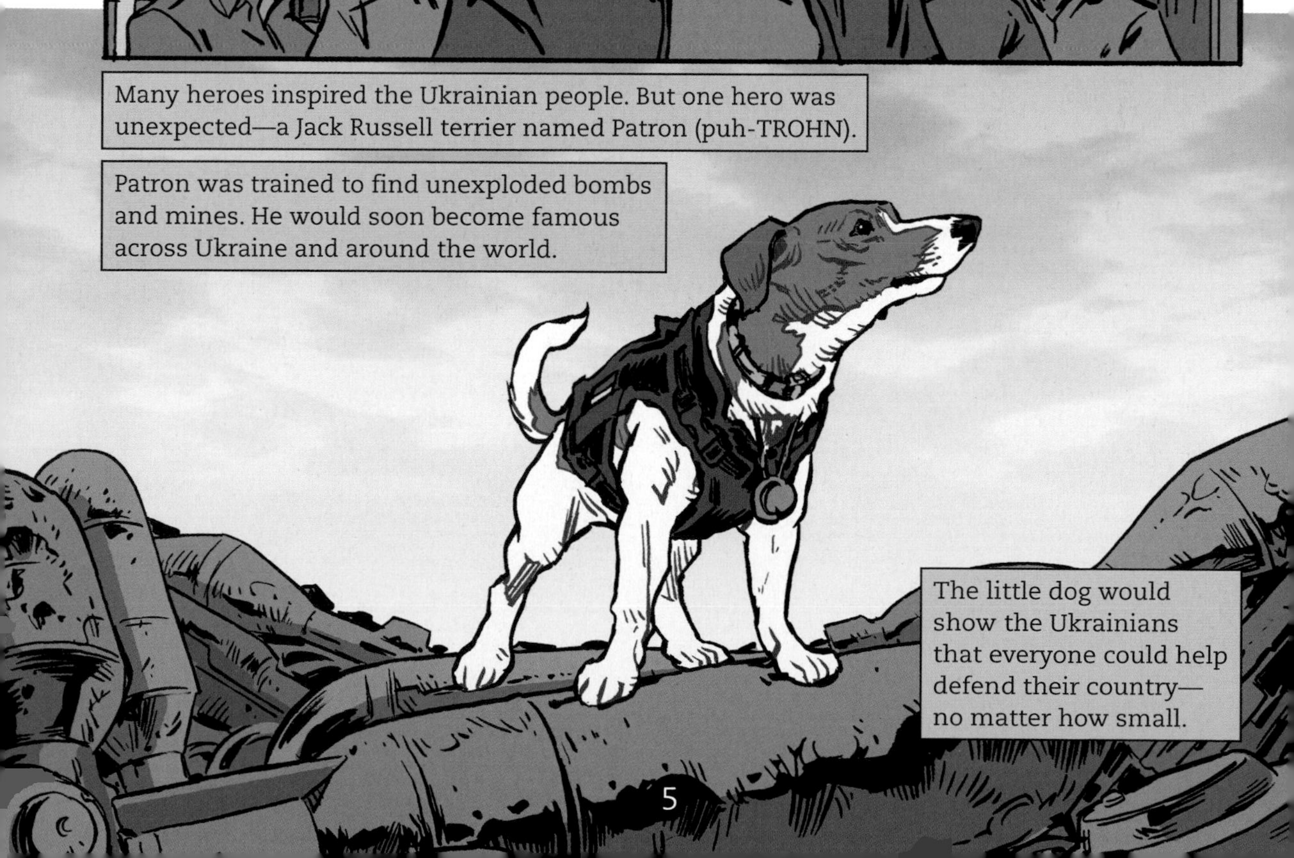
Many heroes inspired the Ukrainian people. But one hero was unexpected—a Jack Russell terrier named Patron (puh-TROHN).
Patron was trained to find unexploded bombs and mines. He would soon become famous across Ukraine and around the world.
The little dog would show the Ukrainians that everyone could help defend their country—no matter how small.

Chapter 2: One Clever Dog

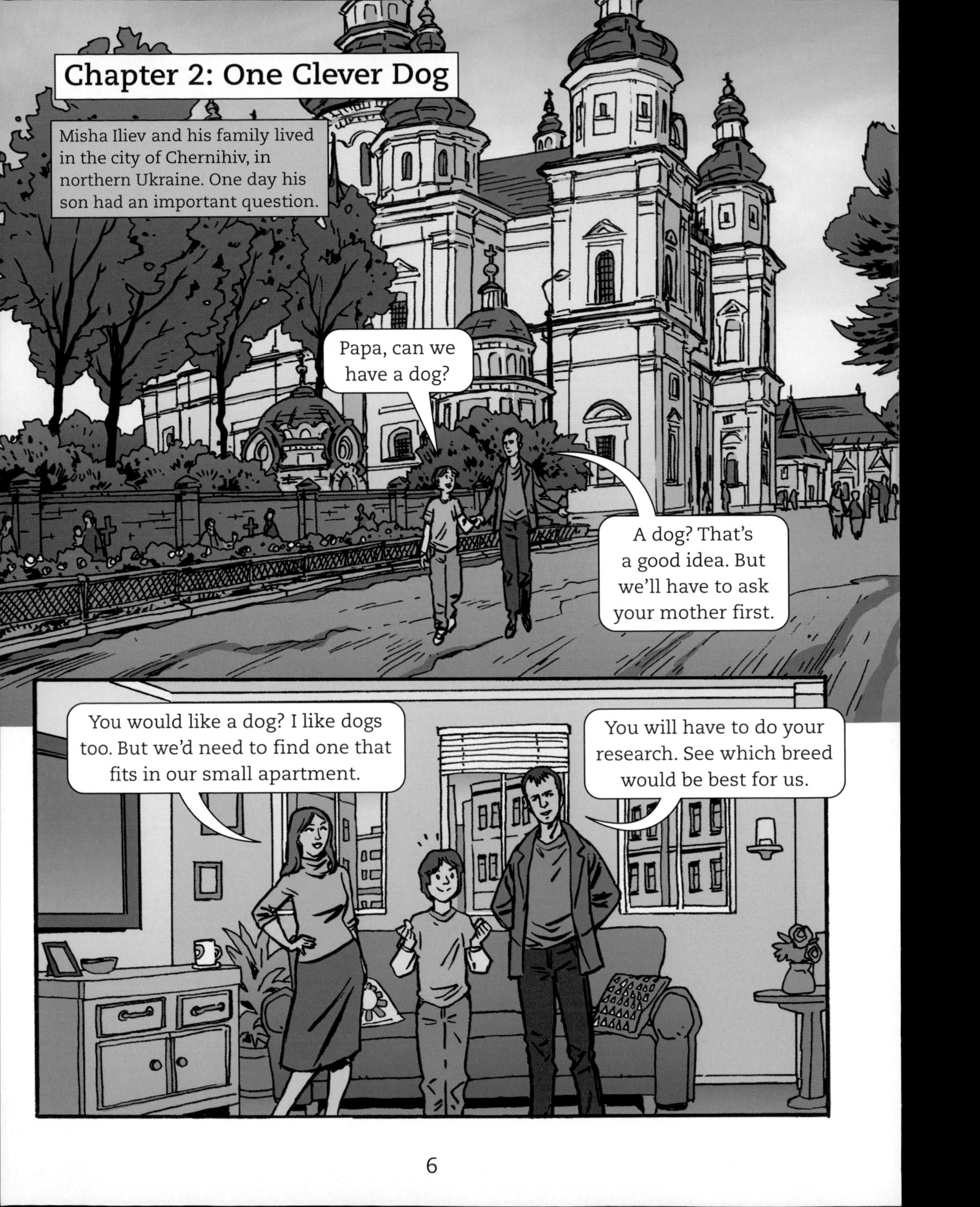
Misha Iliev and his family lived in the city of Chernihiv, in northern Ukraine. One day his son had an important question.
Papa, can we have a dog?
A dog? That's a good idea. But we'll have to ask your mother first.
You would like a dog? I like dogs too. But we'd need to find one that fits in our small apartment.
You will have to do your research. See which breed would be best for us.

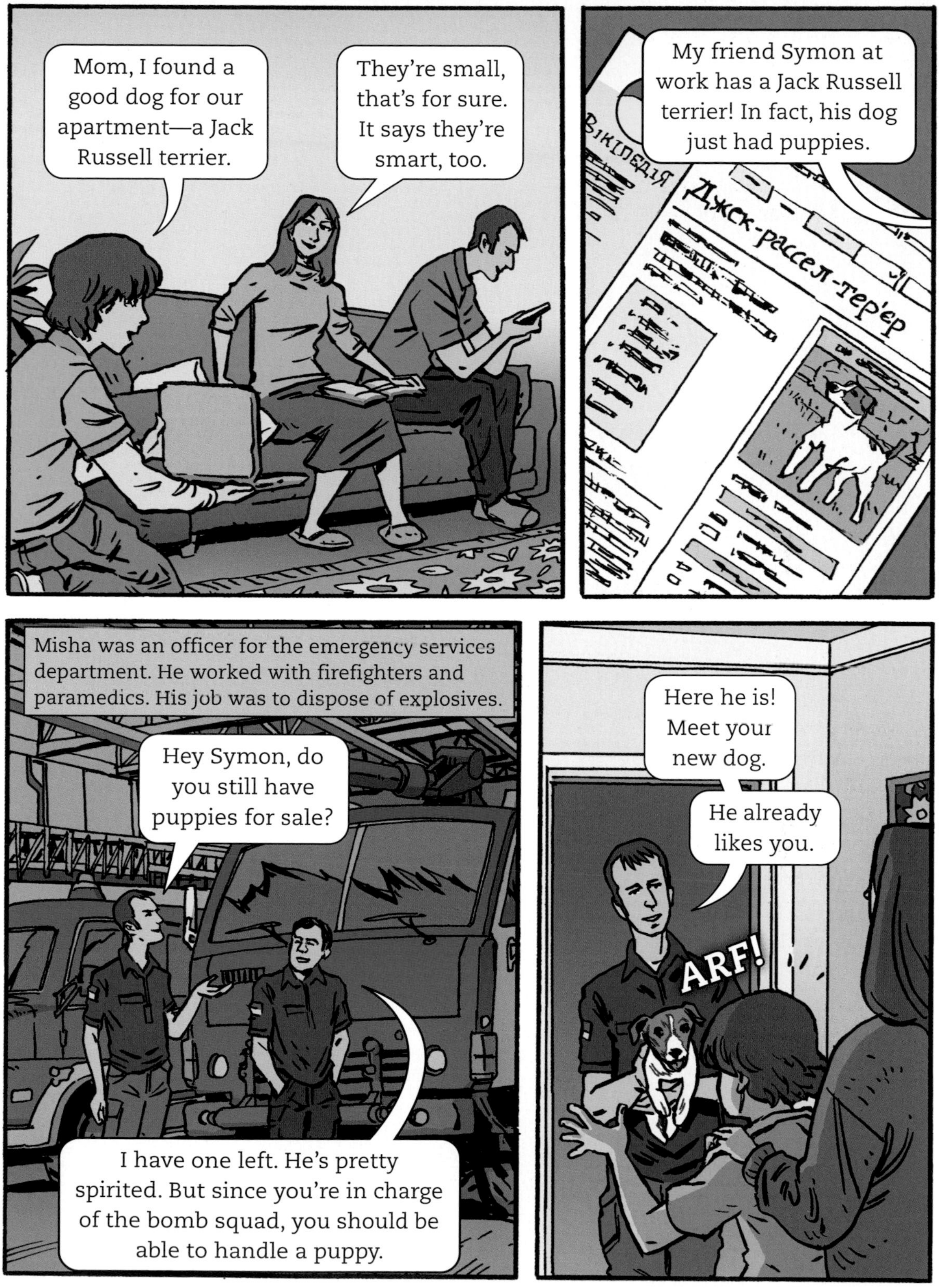
Mom, I found a good dog for our apartment—a Jack Russell terrier.
They're small, that's for sure. It says they're smart, too.
Вікіпедія
Джек-рассел-тер'єр
My friend Symon at work has a Jack Russell terrier! In fact, his dog just had puppies.
Misha was an officer for the emergency services department. He worked with firefighters and paramedics. His job was to dispose of explosives.
Hey Symon, do you still have puppies for sale?
I have one left. He's pretty spirited. But since you're in charge of the bomb squad, you should be able to handle a puppy.
Here he is! Meet your new dog.
He already likes you.
ARF!

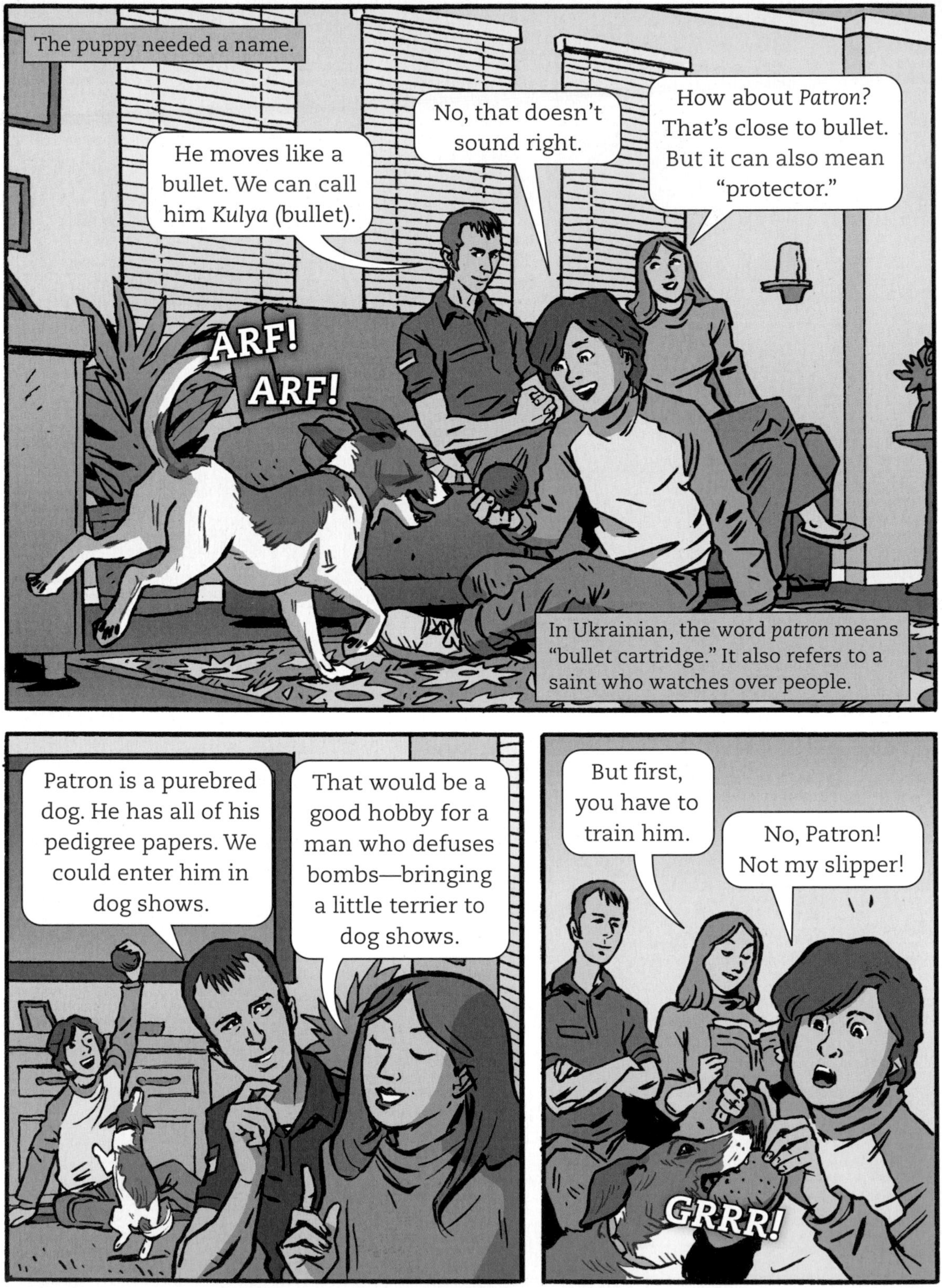
The puppy needed a name.
He moves like a bullet. We can call him *Kulya* (bullet).
No, that doesn't sound right.
How about *Patron*? That's close to bullet. But it can also mean "protector."
ARF!
ARF!
In Ukrainian, the word *patron* means "bullet cartridge." It also refers to a saint who watches over people.
Patron is a purebred dog. He has all of his pedigree papers. We could enter him in dog shows.
That would be a good hobby for a man who defuses bombs—bringing a little terrier to dog shows.
But first, you have to train him.
No, Patron! Not my slipper!
GRRR!

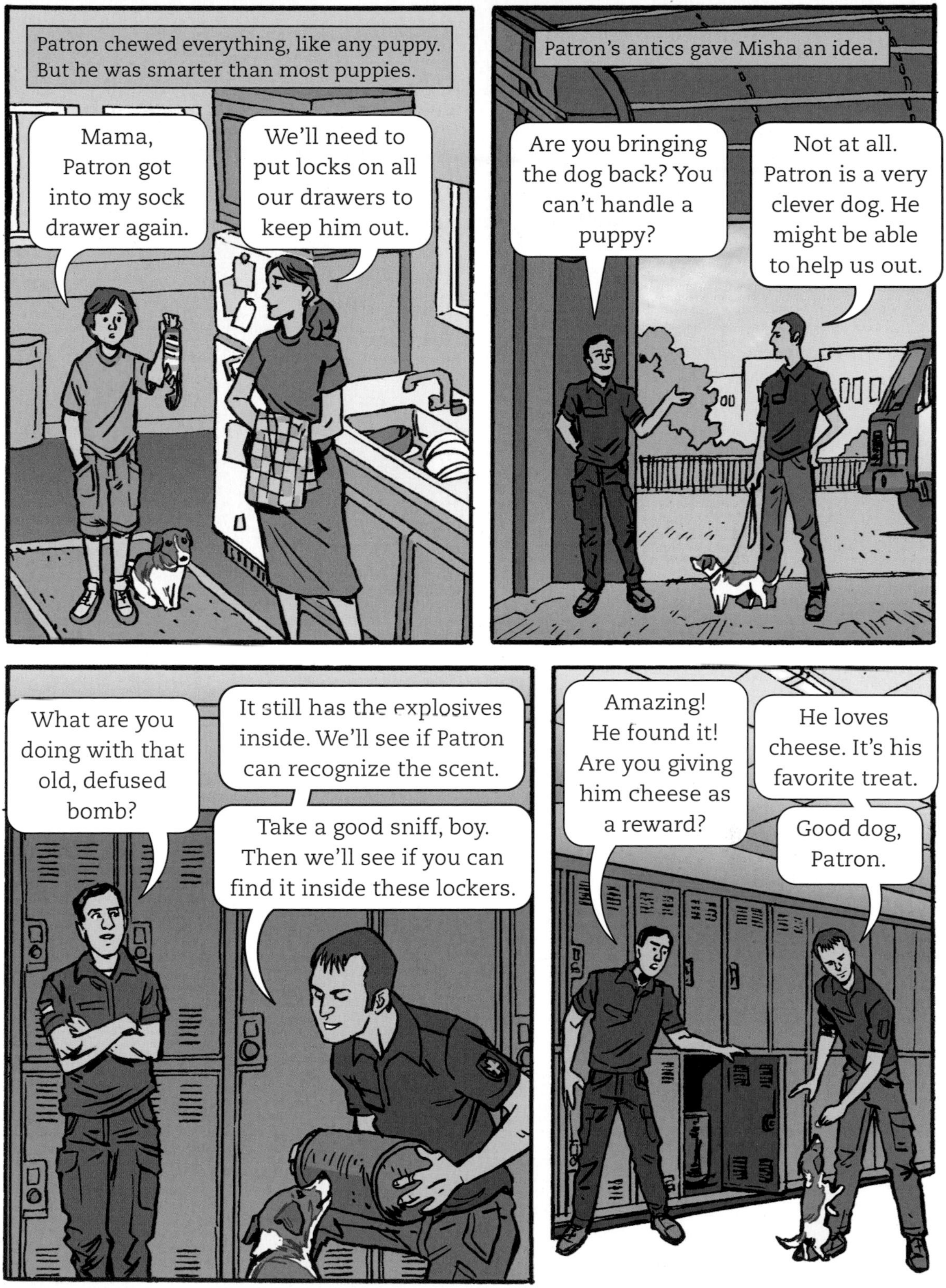

Patron chewed everything, like any puppy. But he was smarter than most puppies.
Mama, Patron got into my sock drawer again.
We'll need to put locks on all our drawers to keep him out.
Patron's antics gave Misha an idea.
Are you bringing the dog back? You can't handle a puppy?
Not at all. Patron is a very clever dog. He might be able to help us out.
What are you doing with that old, defused bomb?
It still has the explosives inside. We'll see if Patron can recognize the scent.
Take a good sniff, boy. Then we'll see if you can find it inside these lockers.
Amazing! He found it! Are you giving him cheese as a reward?
He loves cheese. It's his favorite treat.
Good dog, Patron.

Chapter 3: Guarding Against Danger

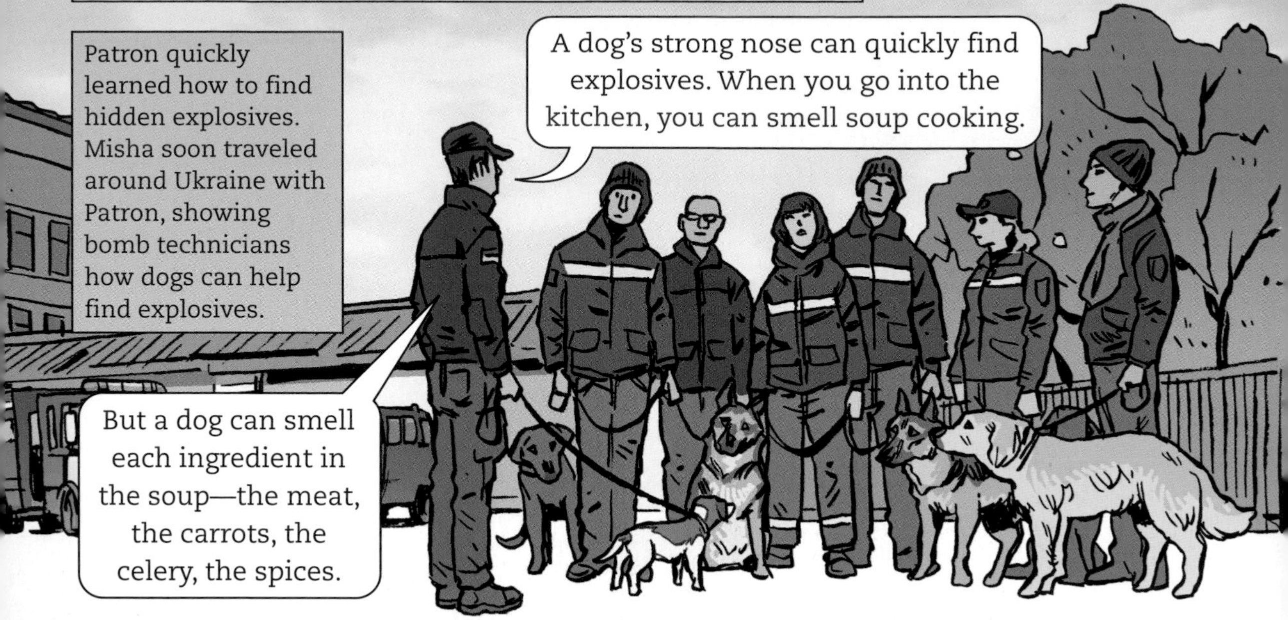
Patron quickly learned how to find hidden explosives. Misha soon traveled around Ukraine with Patron, showing bomb technicians how dogs can help find explosives.
A dog's strong nose can quickly find explosives. When you go into the kitchen, you can smell soup cooking.
But a dog can smell each ingredient in the soup—the meat, the carrots, the celery, the spices.

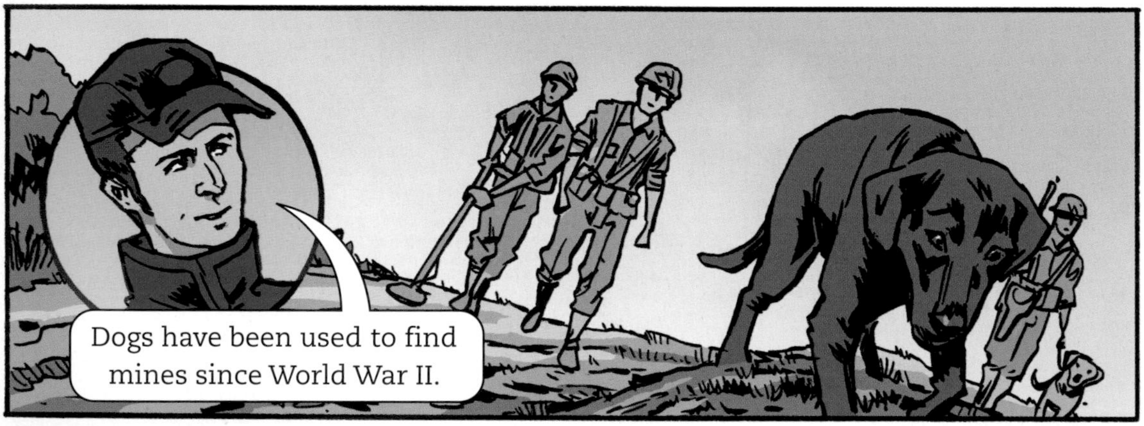
Dogs have been used to find mines since World War II.

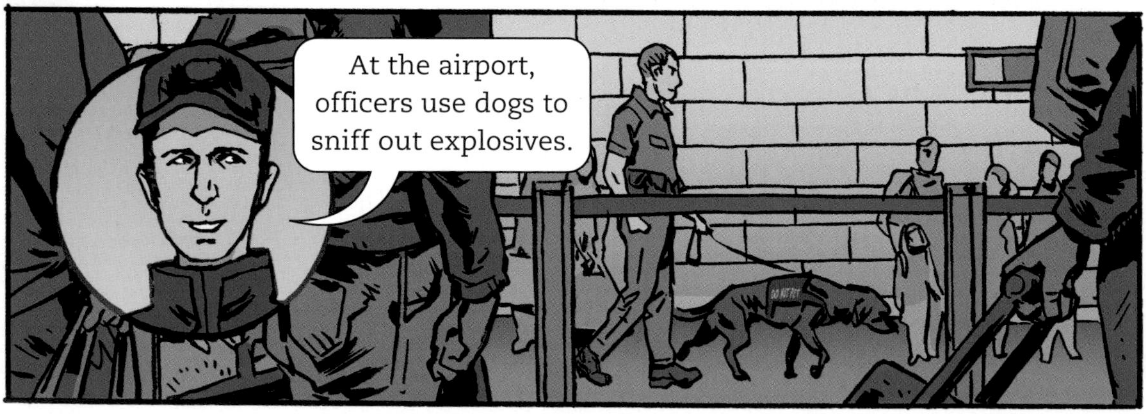
At the airport, officers use dogs to sniff out explosives.

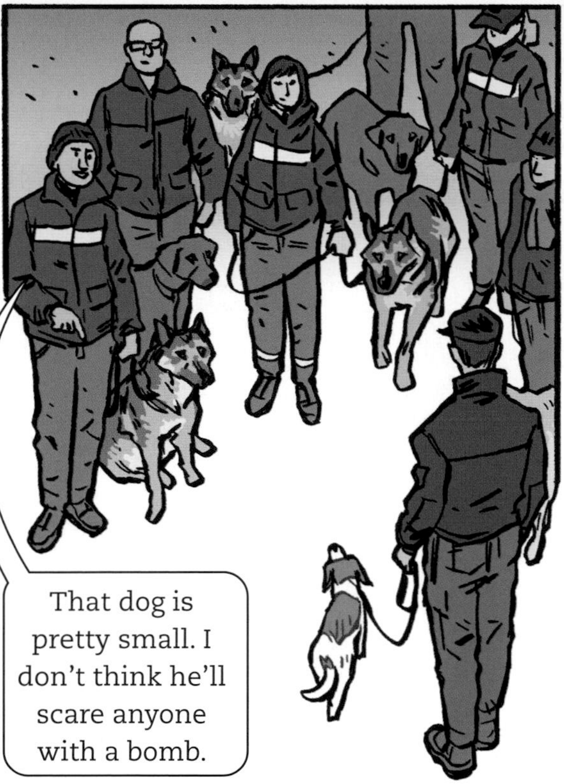
That dog is
pretty small. I
don't think he'll
scare anyone
with a bomb.

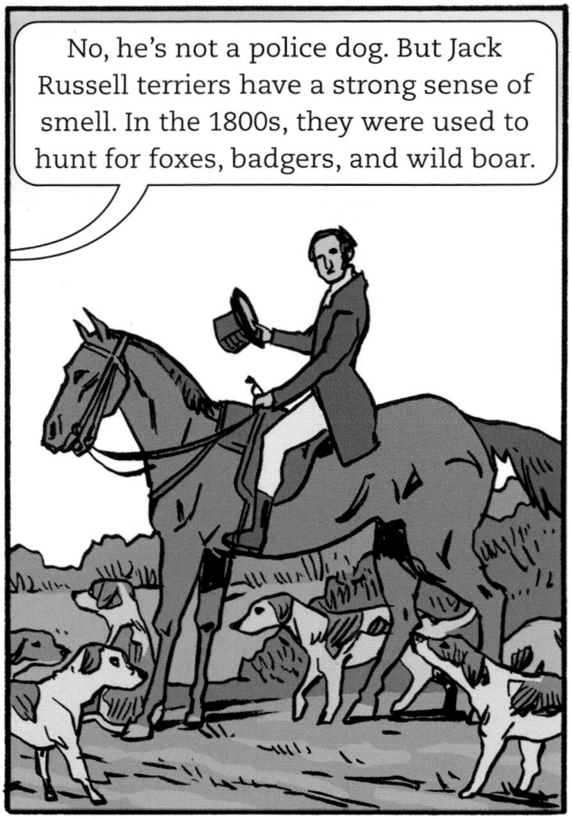
No, he's not a police dog. But Jack
Russell terriers have a strong sense of
smell. In the 1800s, they were used to
hunt for foxes, badgers, and wild boar.

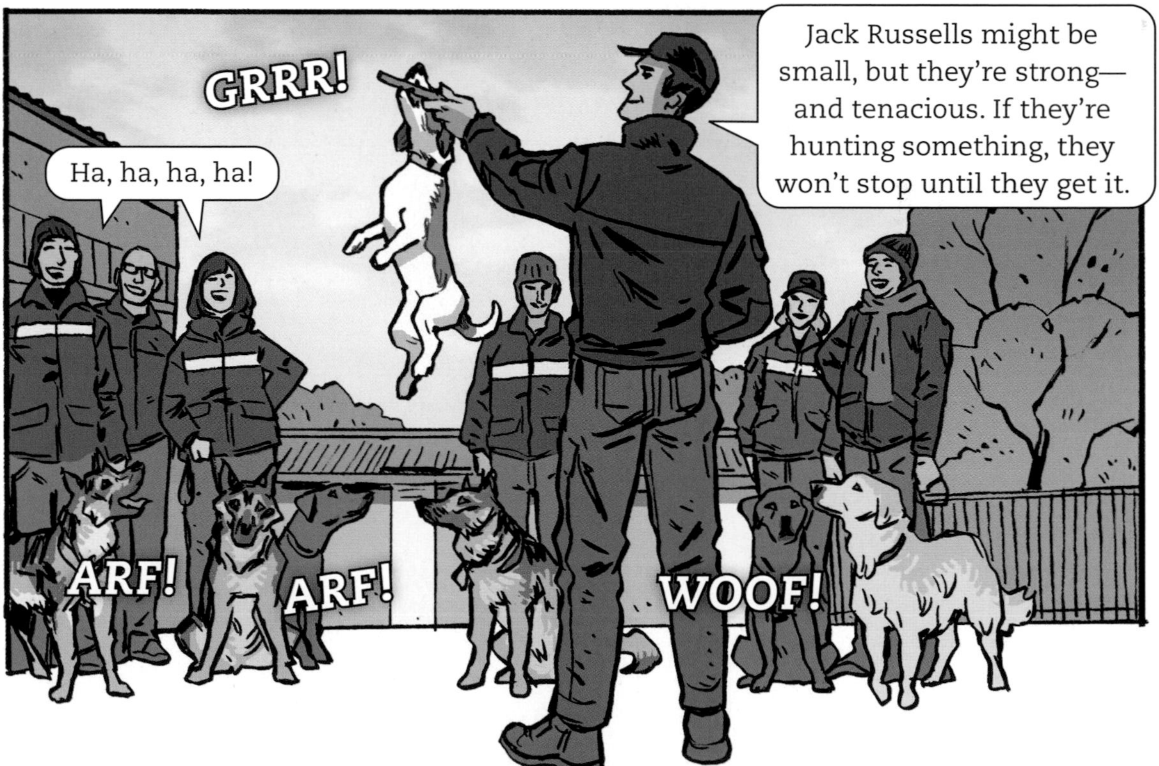
GRRR!
Jack Russells might be
small, but they're strong—
and tenacious. If they're
hunting something, they
won't stop until they get it.
Ha, ha, ha, ha!
ARF!
ARF!
WOOF!

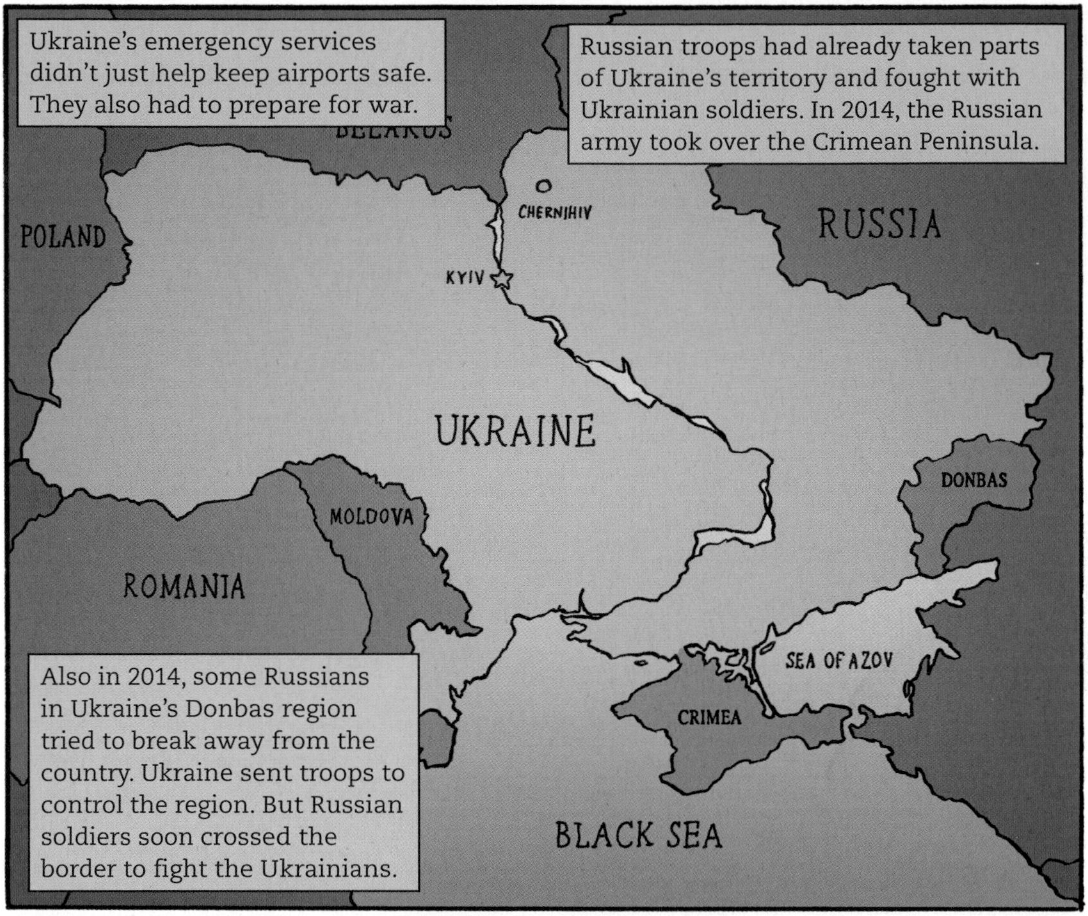
Ukraine's emergency services didn't just help keep airports safe. They also had to prepare for war.
Russian troops had already taken parts of Ukraine's territory and fought with Ukrainian soldiers. In 2014, the Russian army took over the Crimean Peninsula.
BELARUS
POLAND
CHERNIHIV
KYIV
RUSSIA
UKRAINE
DONBAS
MOLDOVA
ROMANIA
SEA OF AZOV
CRIMEA
BLACK SEA
Also in 2014, some Russians in Ukraine's Donbas region tried to break away from the country. Ukraine sent troops to control the region. But Russian soldiers soon crossed the border to fight the Ukrainians.

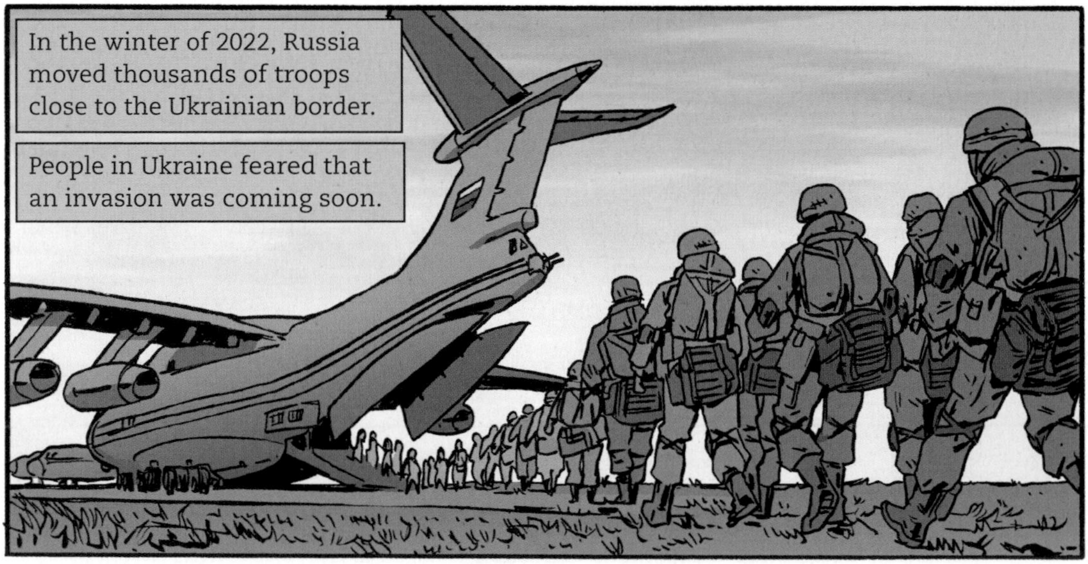
In the winter of 2022, Russia moved thousands of troops close to the Ukrainian border.
People in Ukraine feared that an invasion was coming soon.

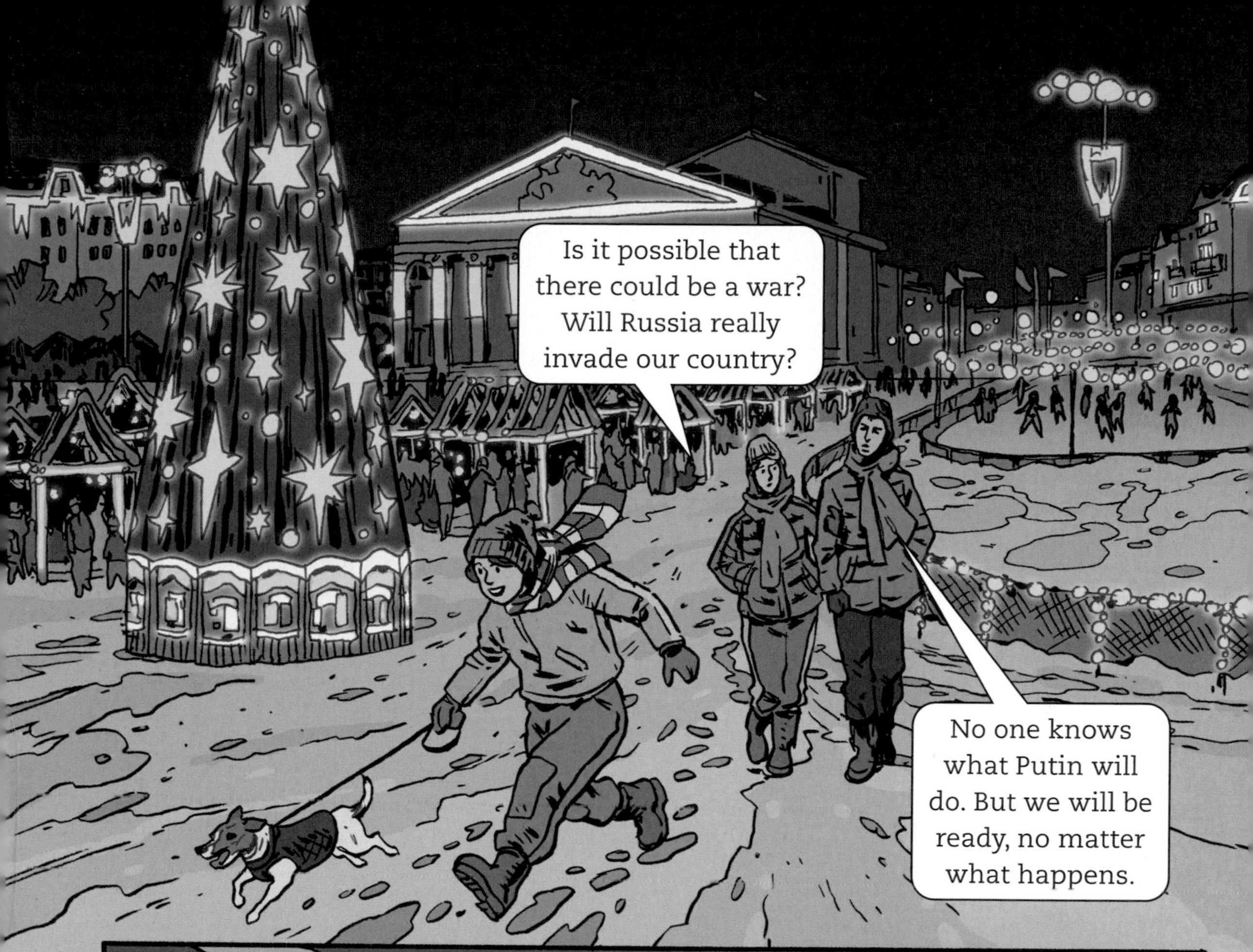
Is it possible that there could be a war? Will Russia really invade our country?
No one knows what Putin will do. But we will be ready, no matter what happens.

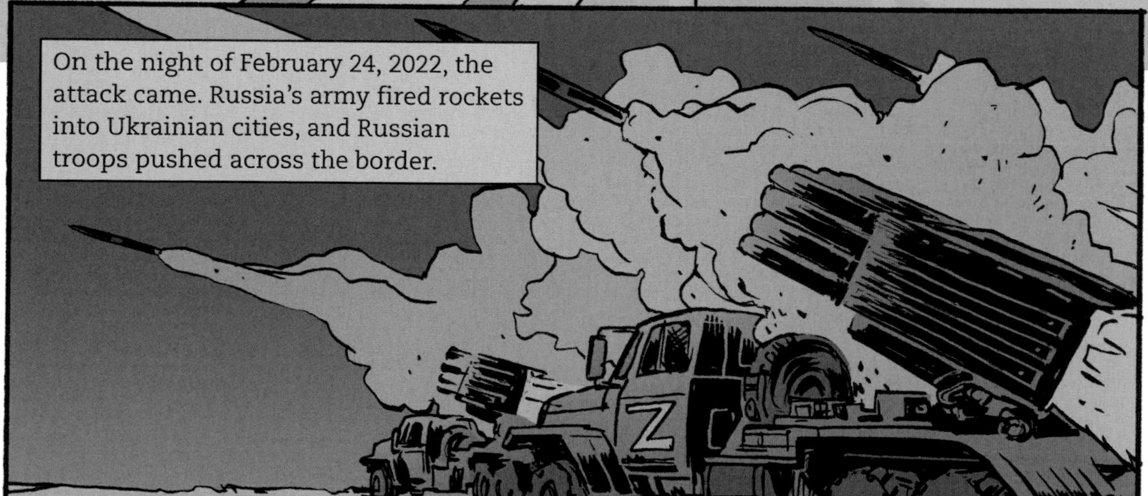
On the night of February 24, 2022, the attack came. Russia's army fired rockets into Ukrainian cities, and Russian troops pushed across the border.

Chapter 4: Invasion!

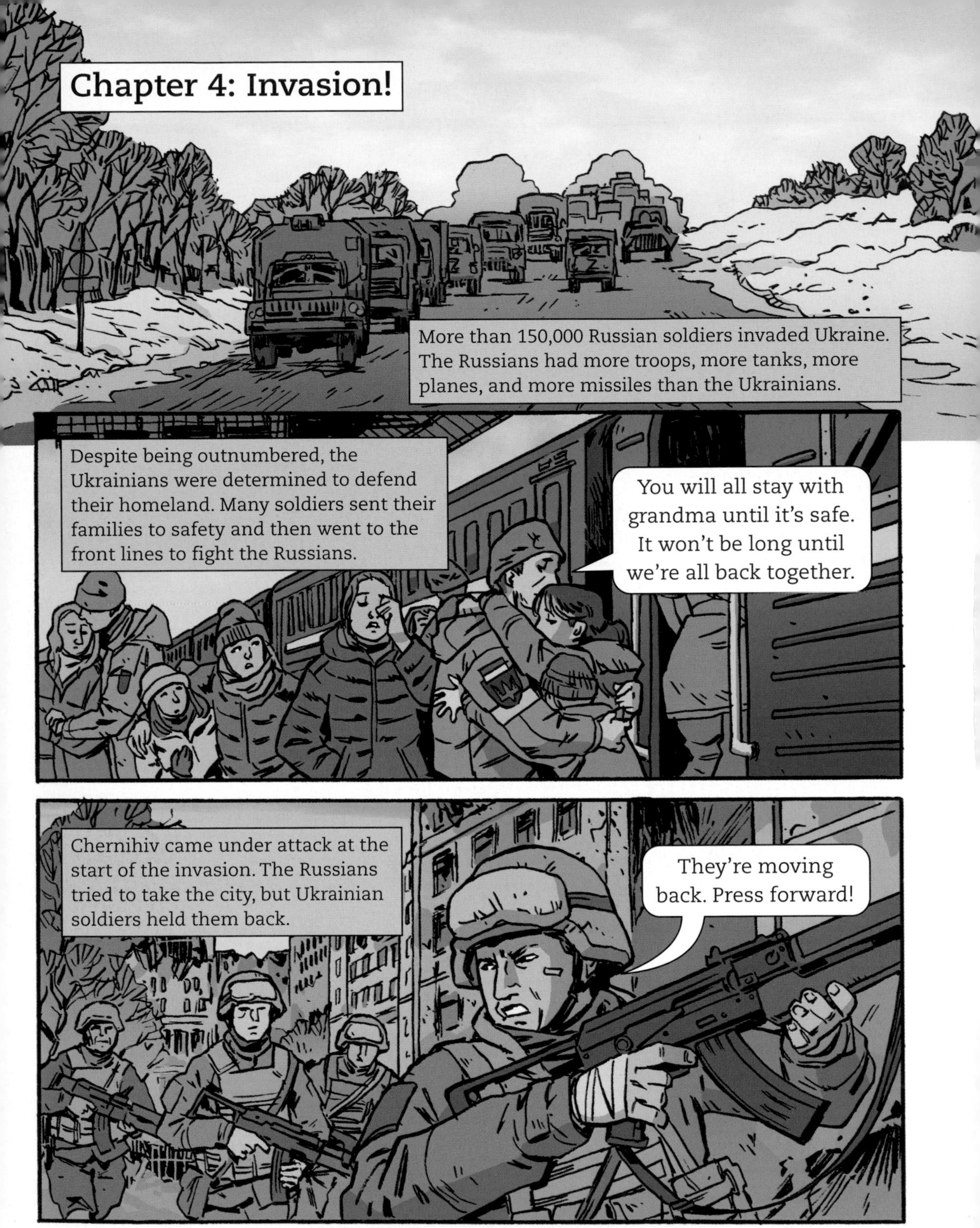

More than 150,000 Russian soldiers invaded Ukraine. The Russians had more troops, more tanks, more planes, and more missiles than the Ukrainians.
Despite being outnumbered, the Ukrainians were determined to defend their homeland. Many soldiers sent their families to safety and then went to the front lines to fight the Russians.
You will all stay with grandma until it's safe. It won't be long until we're all back together.
Chernihiv came under attack at the start of the invasion. The Russians tried to take the city, but Ukrainian soldiers held them back.
They're moving back. Press forward!

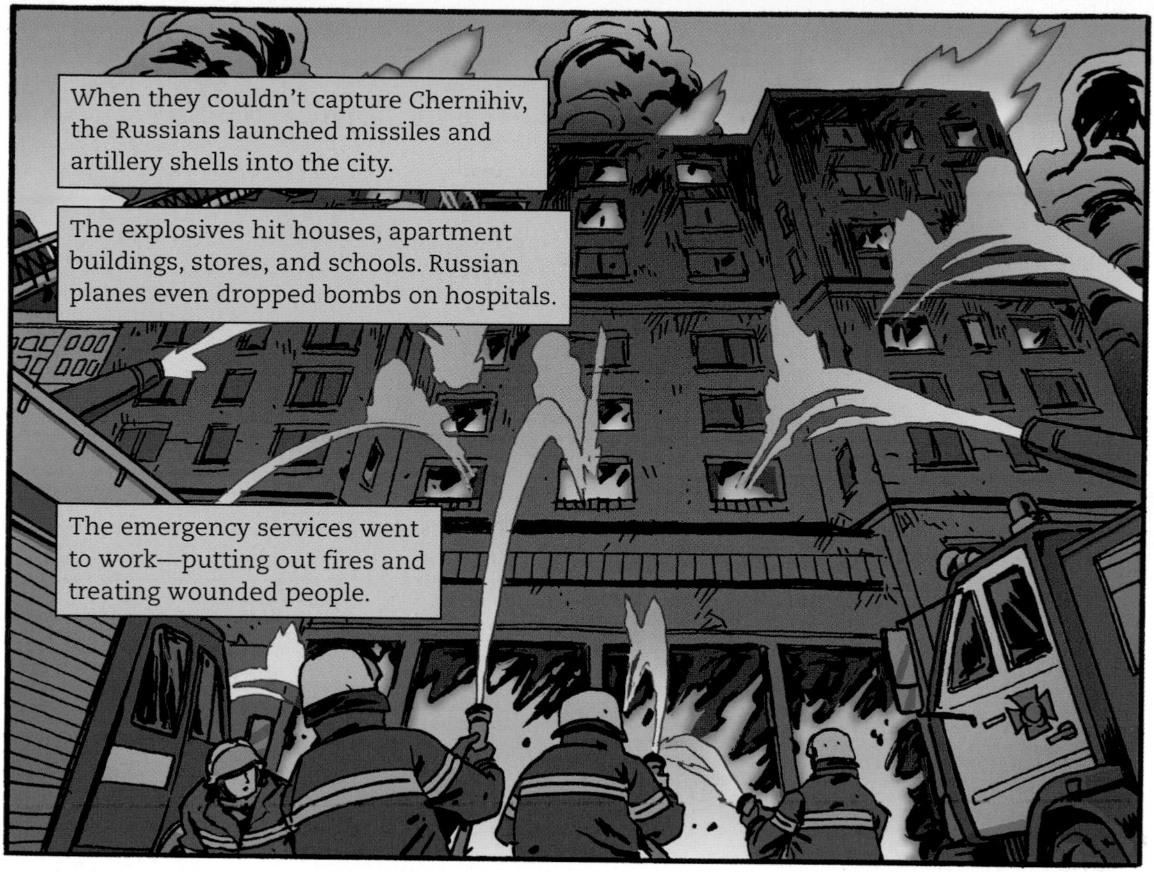
When they couldn't capture Chernihiv, the Russians launched missiles and artillery shells into the city.
The explosives hit houses, apartment buildings, stores, and schools. Russian planes even dropped bombs on hospitals.
The emergency services went to work—putting out fires and treating wounded people.

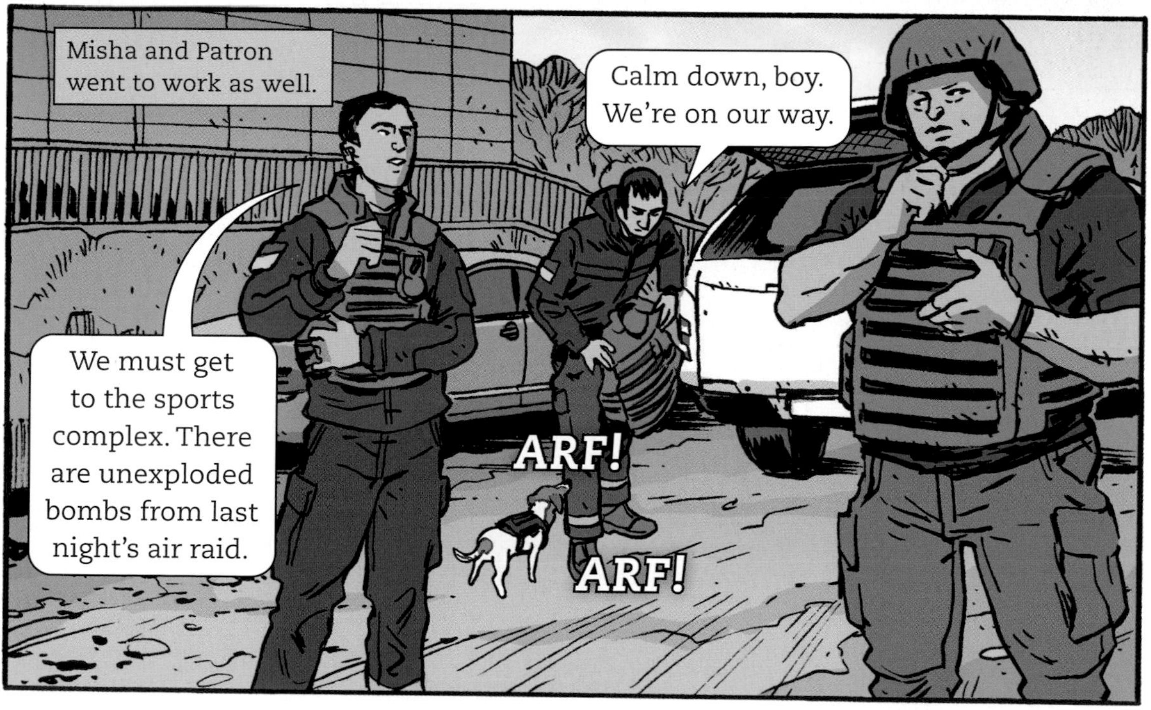
Misha and Patron went to work as well.
We must get to the sports complex. There are unexploded bombs from last night's air raid.
Calm down, boy. We're on our way.
ARF!
ARF!

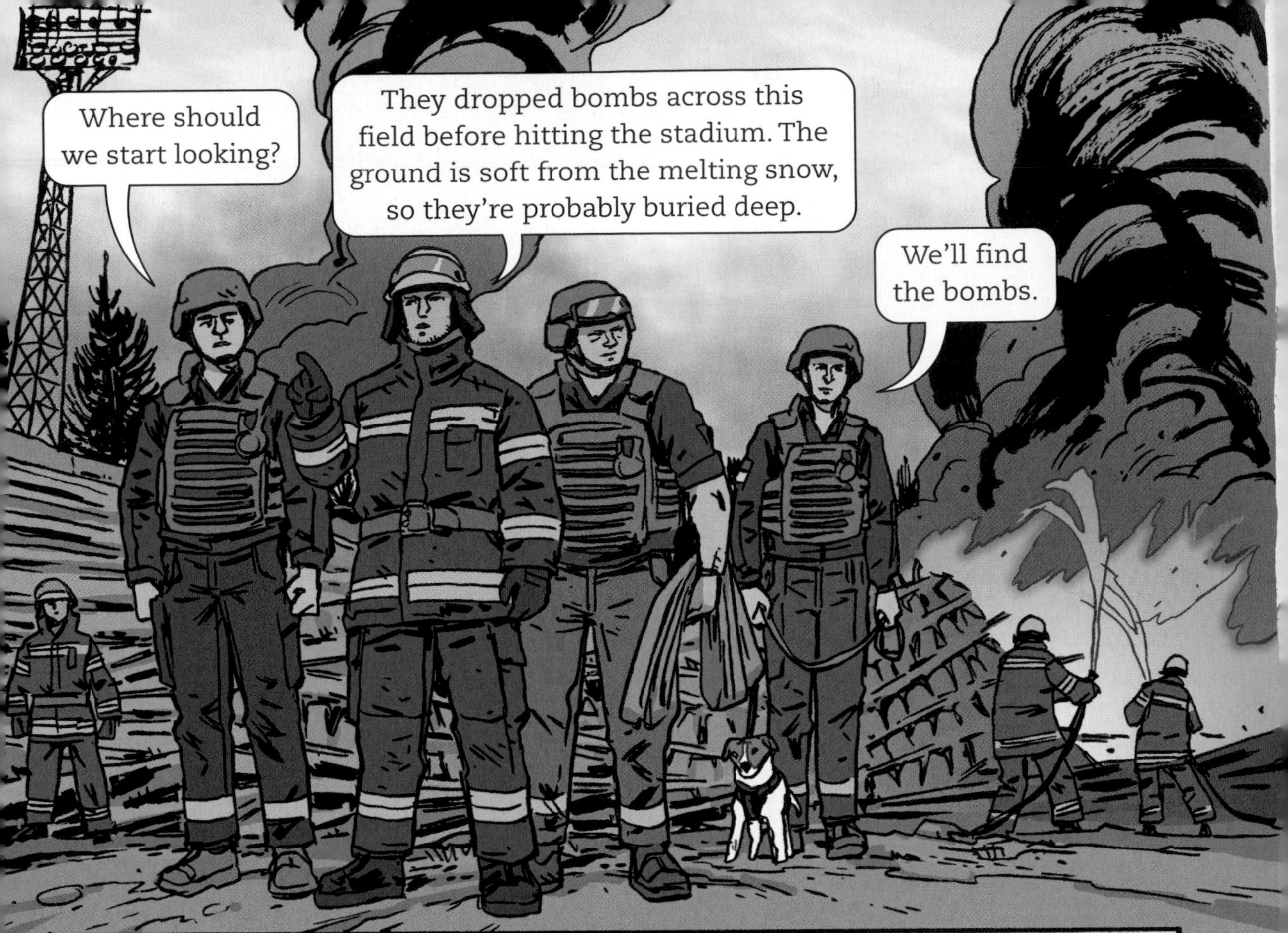
Where should we start looking?
They dropped bombs across this field before hitting the stadium. The ground is soft from the melting snow, so they're probably buried deep.
We'll find the bombs.

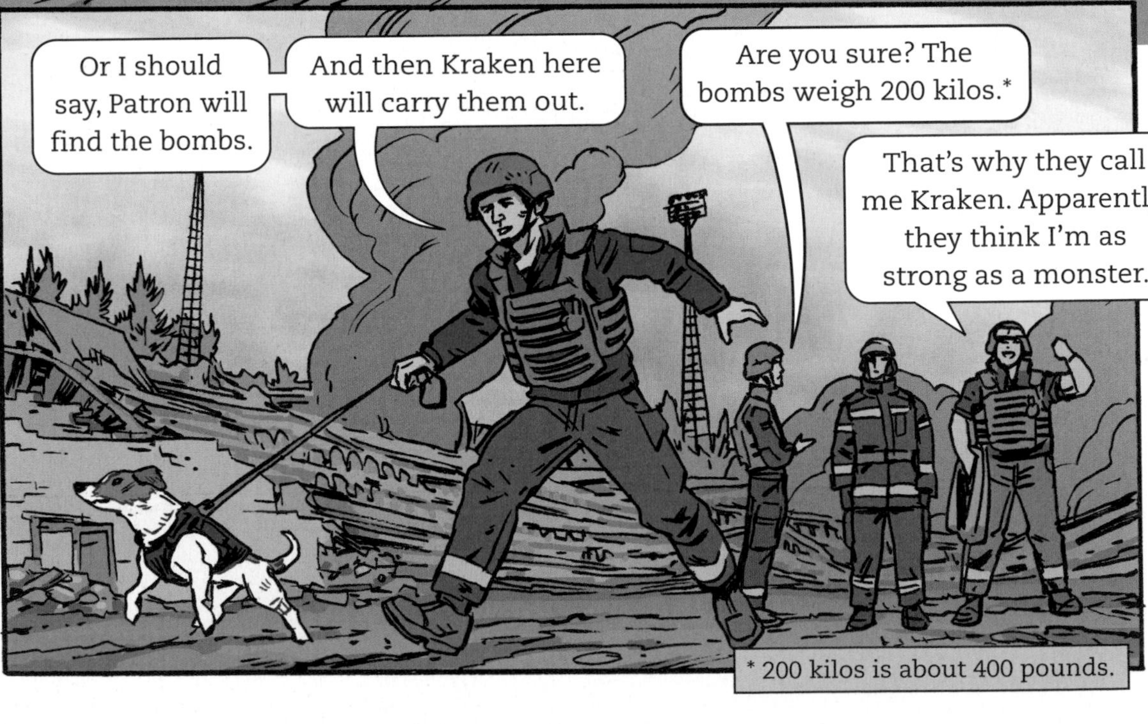
Or I should say, Patron will find the bombs.
And then Kraken here will carry them out.
Are you sure? The bombs weigh 200 kilos.*
That's why they call me Kraken. Apparently, they think I'm as strong as a monster.

* 200 kilos is about 400 pounds.

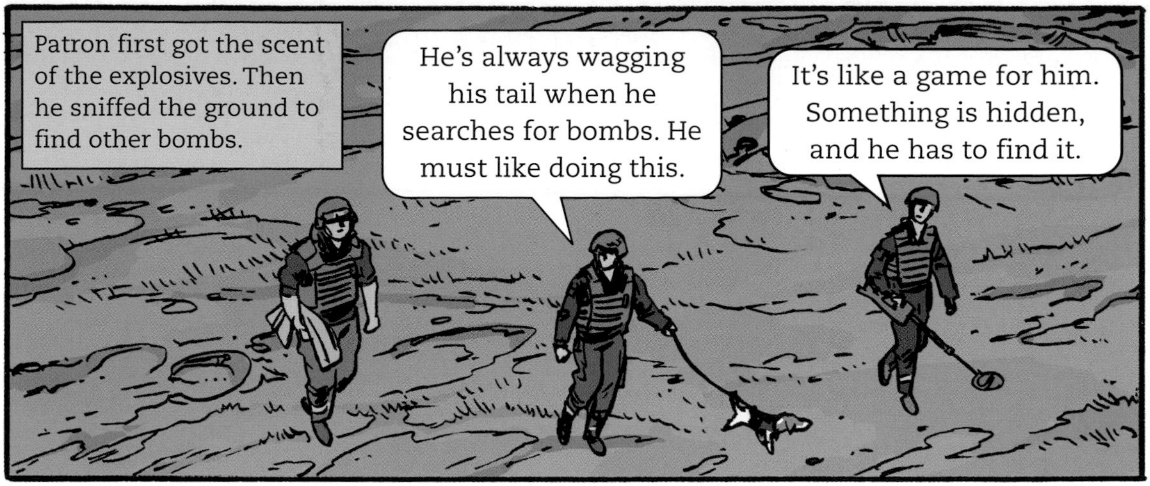
Patron first got the scent of the explosives. Then he sniffed the ground to find other bombs.
He's always wagging his tail when he searches for bombs. He must like doing this.
It's like a game for him. Something is hidden, and he has to find it.

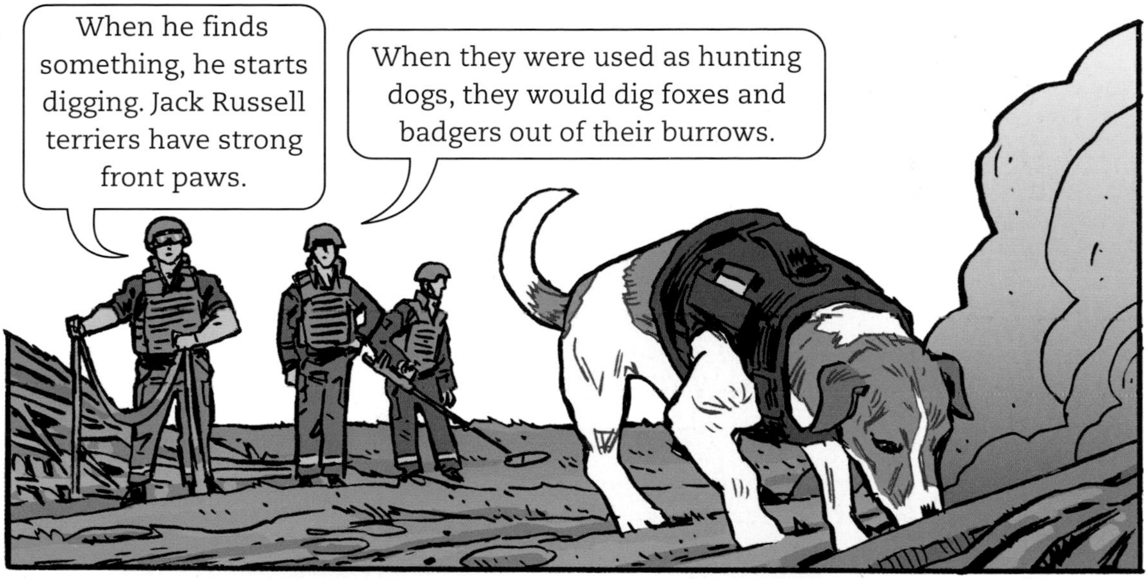
When he finds something, he starts digging. Jack Russell terriers have strong front paws.
When they were used as hunting dogs, they would dig foxes and badgers out of their burrows.

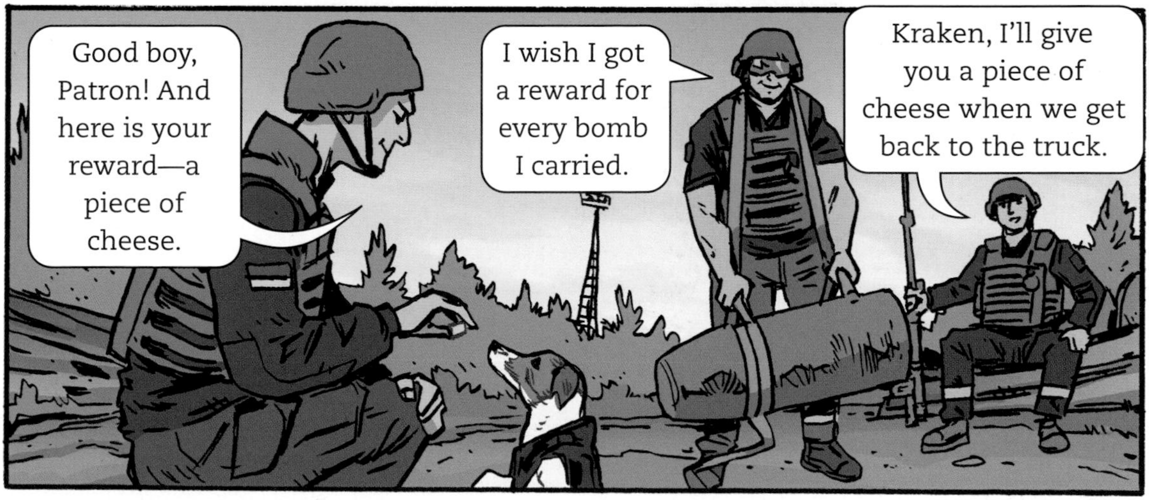
Good boy, Patron! And here is your reward—a piece of cheese.
I wish I got a reward for every bomb I carried.
Kraken, I'll give you a piece of cheese when we get back to the truck.

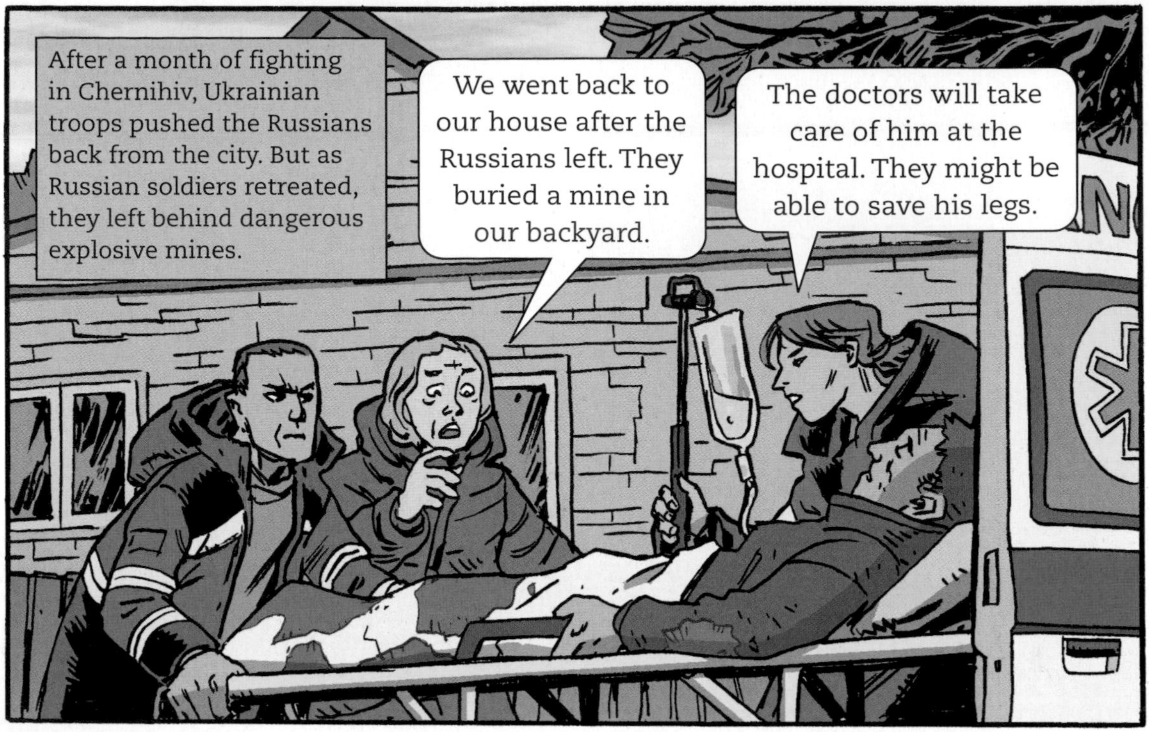
After a month of fighting in Chernihiv, Ukrainian troops pushed the Russians back from the city. But as Russian soldiers retreated, they left behind dangerous explosive mines.
We went back to our house after the Russians left. They buried a mine in our backyard.
The doctors will take care of him at the hospital. They might be able to save his legs.

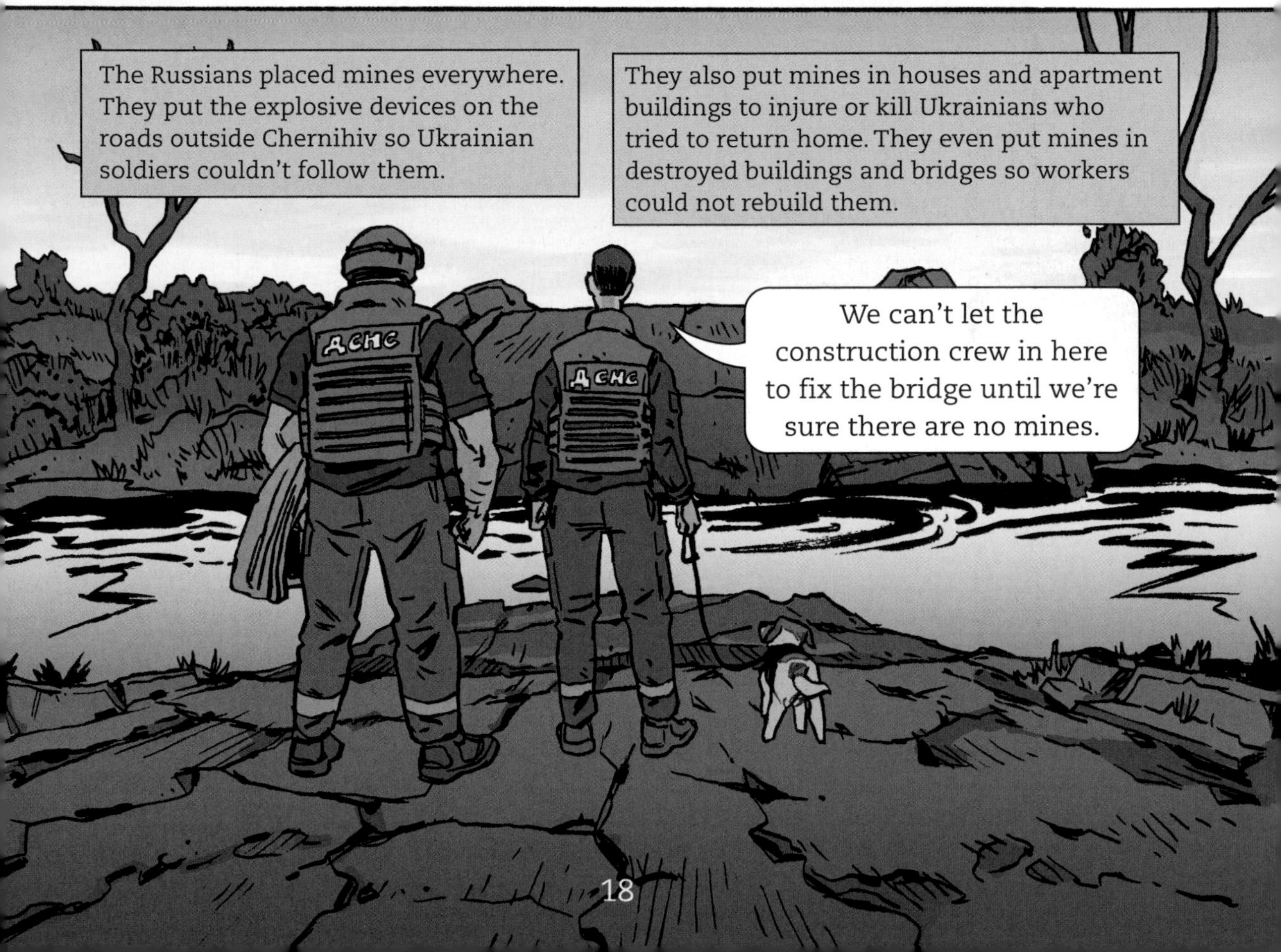
The Russians placed mines everywhere. They put the explosive devices on the roads outside Chernihiv so Ukrainian soldiers couldn't follow them.
They also put mines in houses and apartment buildings to injure or kill Ukrainians who tried to return home. They even put mines in destroyed buildings and bridges so workers could not rebuild them.
ДСНС
ДСНС
We can't let the construction crew in here to fix the bridge until we're sure there are no mines.

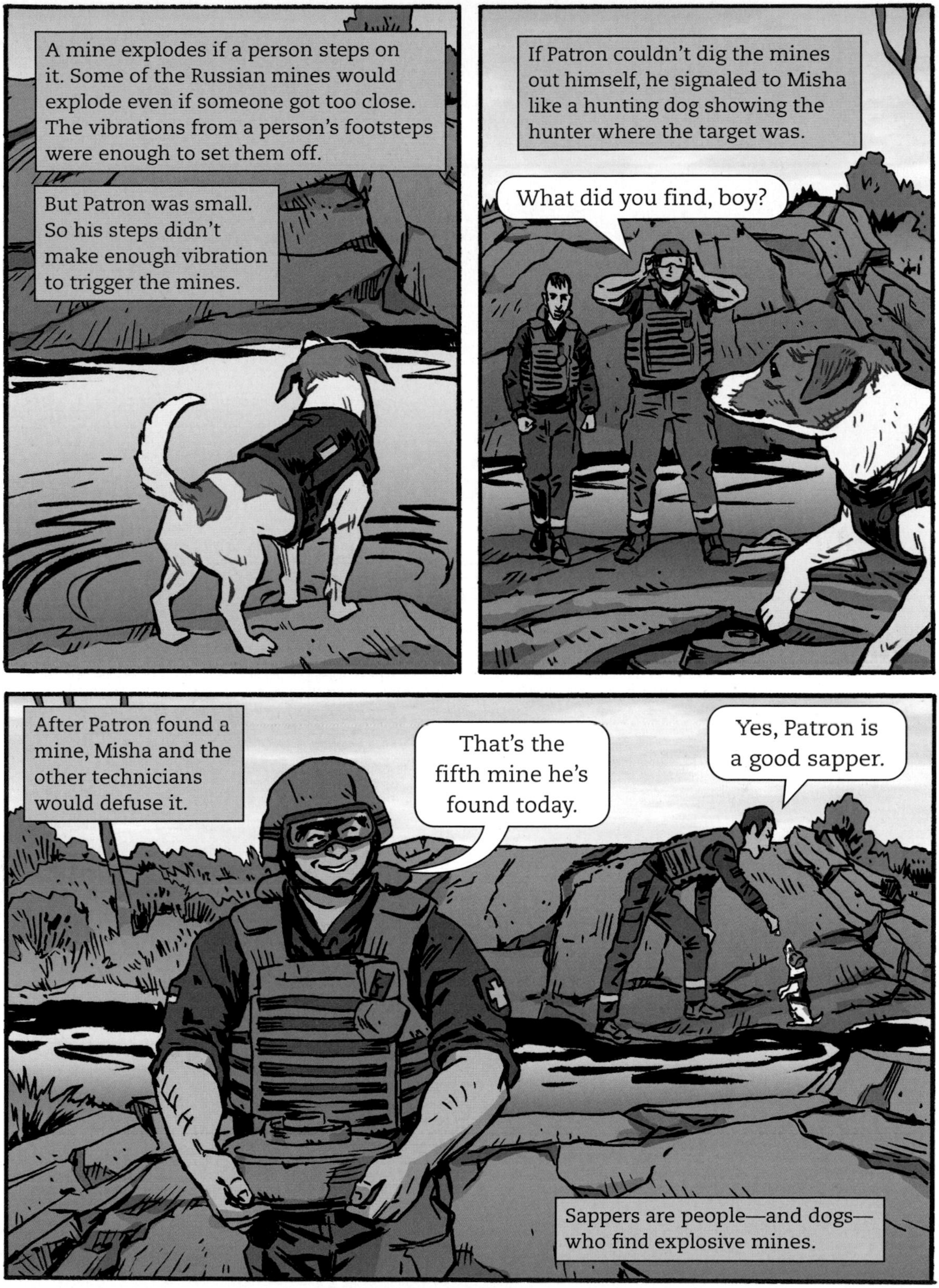
A mine explodes if a person steps on it. Some of the Russian mines would explode even if someone got too close. The vibrations from a person's footsteps were enough to set them off.
But Patron was small. So his steps didn't make enough vibration to trigger the mines.
If Patron couldn't dig the mines out himself, he signaled to Misha like a hunting dog showing the hunter where the target was.
What did you find, boy?
After Patron found a mine, Misha and the other technicians would defuse it.
That's the fifth mine he's found today.
Yes, Patron is a good sapper.
Sappers are people—and dogs—who find explosive mines.

Chapter 5: Keeping Children Safe

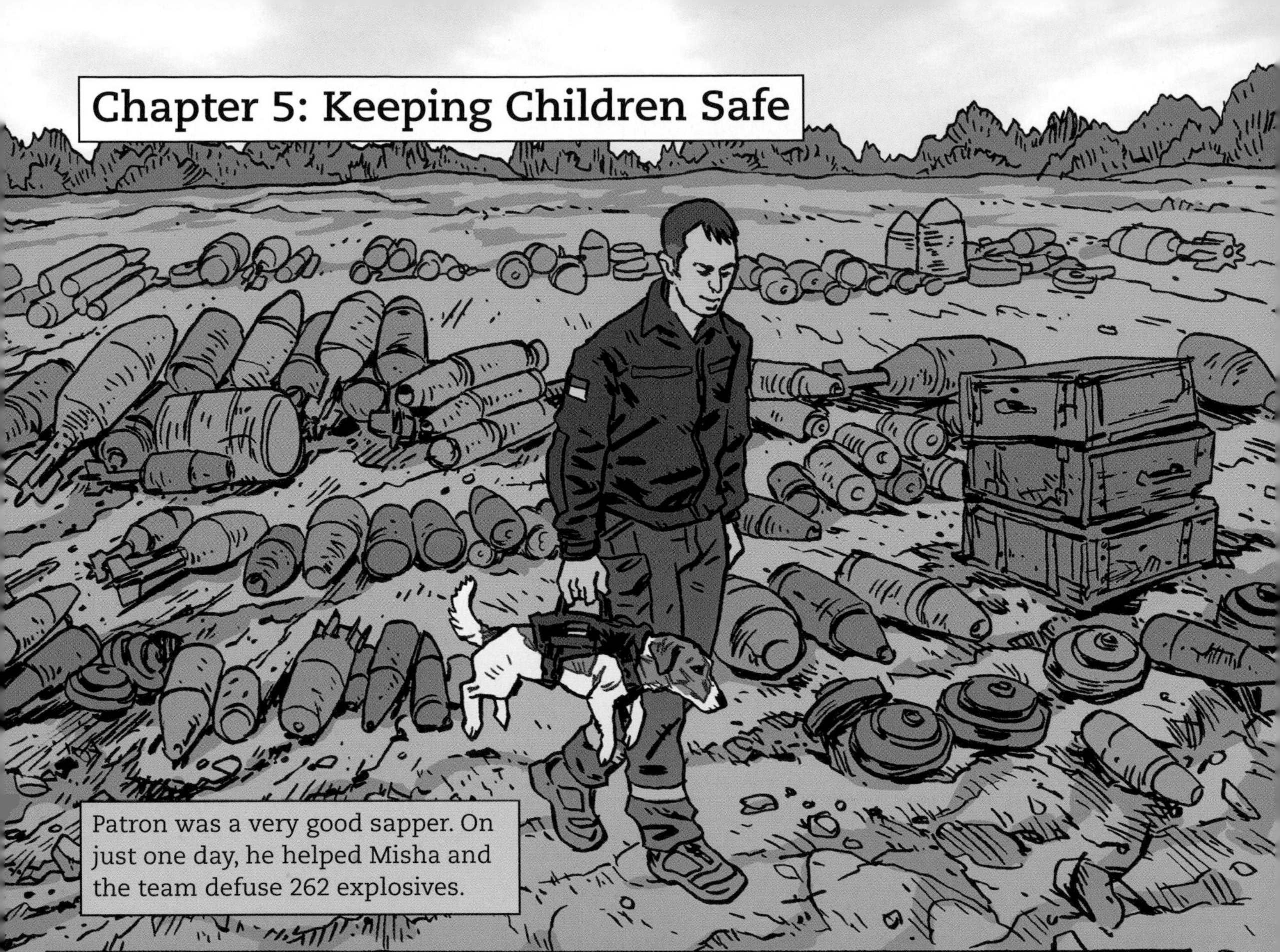

Patron was a very good sapper. On just one day, he helped Misha and the team defuse 262 explosives.

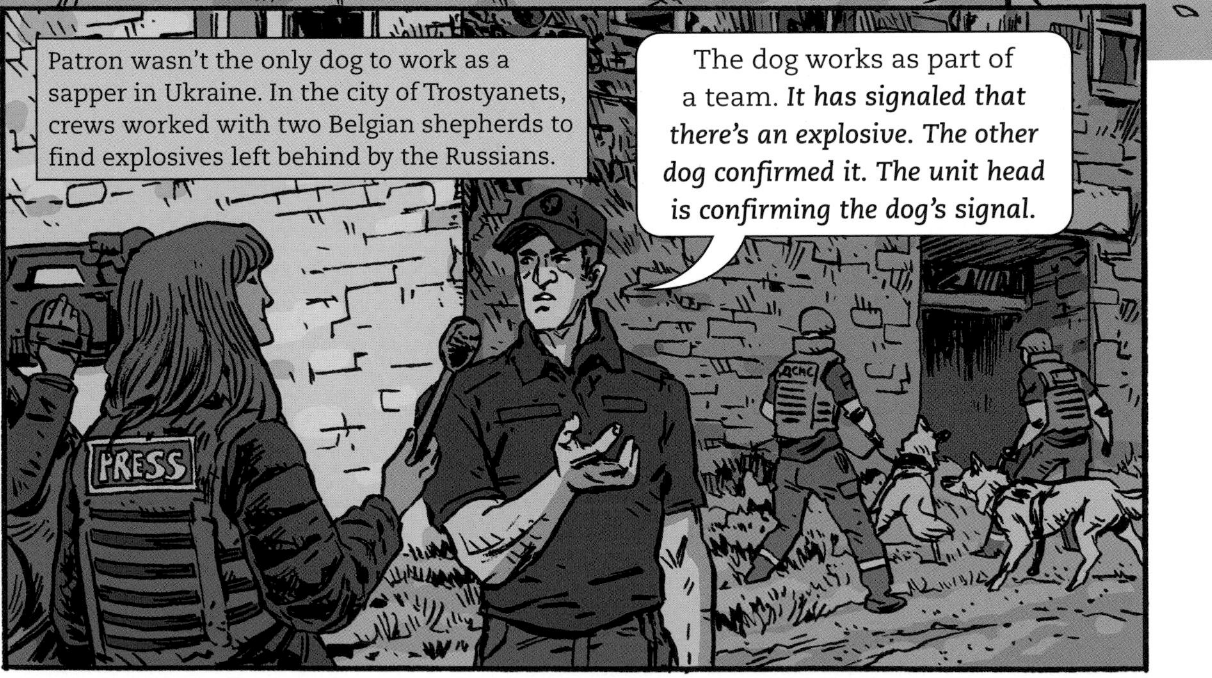

Patron wasn't the only dog to work as a sapper in Ukraine. In the city of Trostyanets, crews worked with two Belgian shepherds to find explosives left behind by the Russians.
The dog works as part of a team. *It has signaled that there's an explosive. The other dog confirmed it. The unit head is confirming the dog's signal.*
PRESS

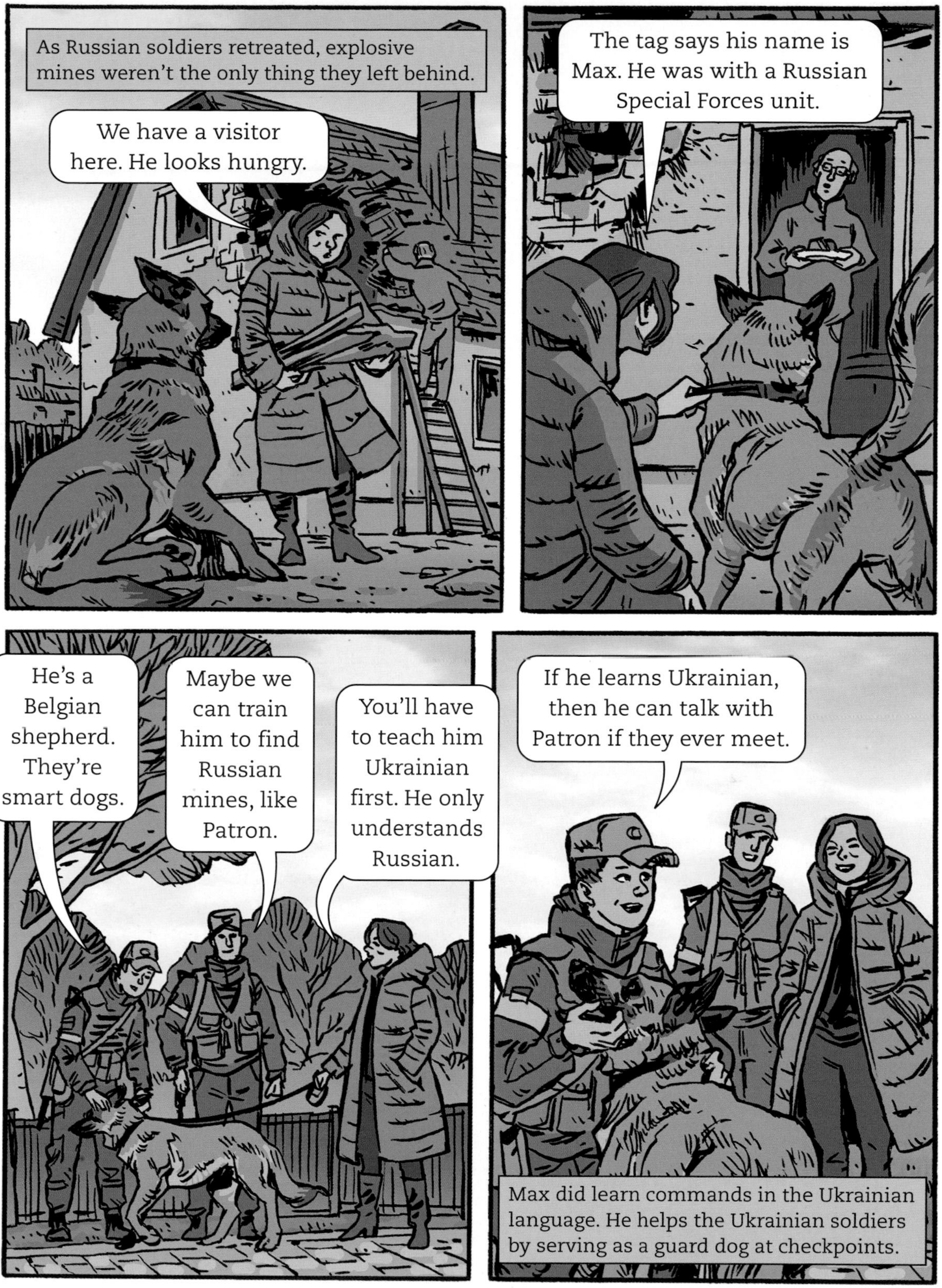
As Russian soldiers retreated, explosive mines weren't the only thing they left behind.
We have a visitor here. He looks hungry.
The tag says his name is Max. He was with a Russian Special Forces unit.
He's a Belgian shepherd. They're smart dogs.
Maybe we can train him to find Russian mines, like Patron.
You'll have to teach him Ukrainian first. He only understands Russian.
If he learns Ukrainian, then he can talk with Patron if they ever meet.
Max did learn commands in the Ukrainian language. He helps the Ukrainian soldiers by serving as a guard dog at checkpoints.

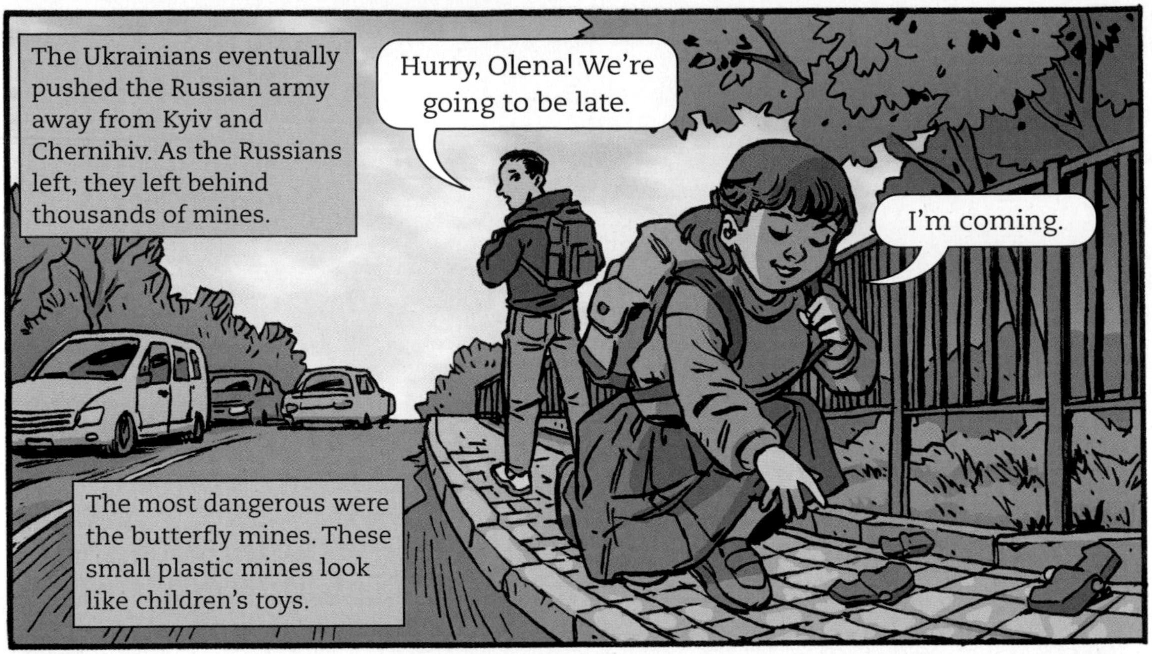
The Ukrainians eventually pushed the Russian army away from Kyiv and Chernihiv. As the Russians left, they left behind thousands of mines.
Hurry, Olena! We're going to be late.
I'm coming.
The most dangerous were the butterfly mines. These small plastic mines look like children's toys.

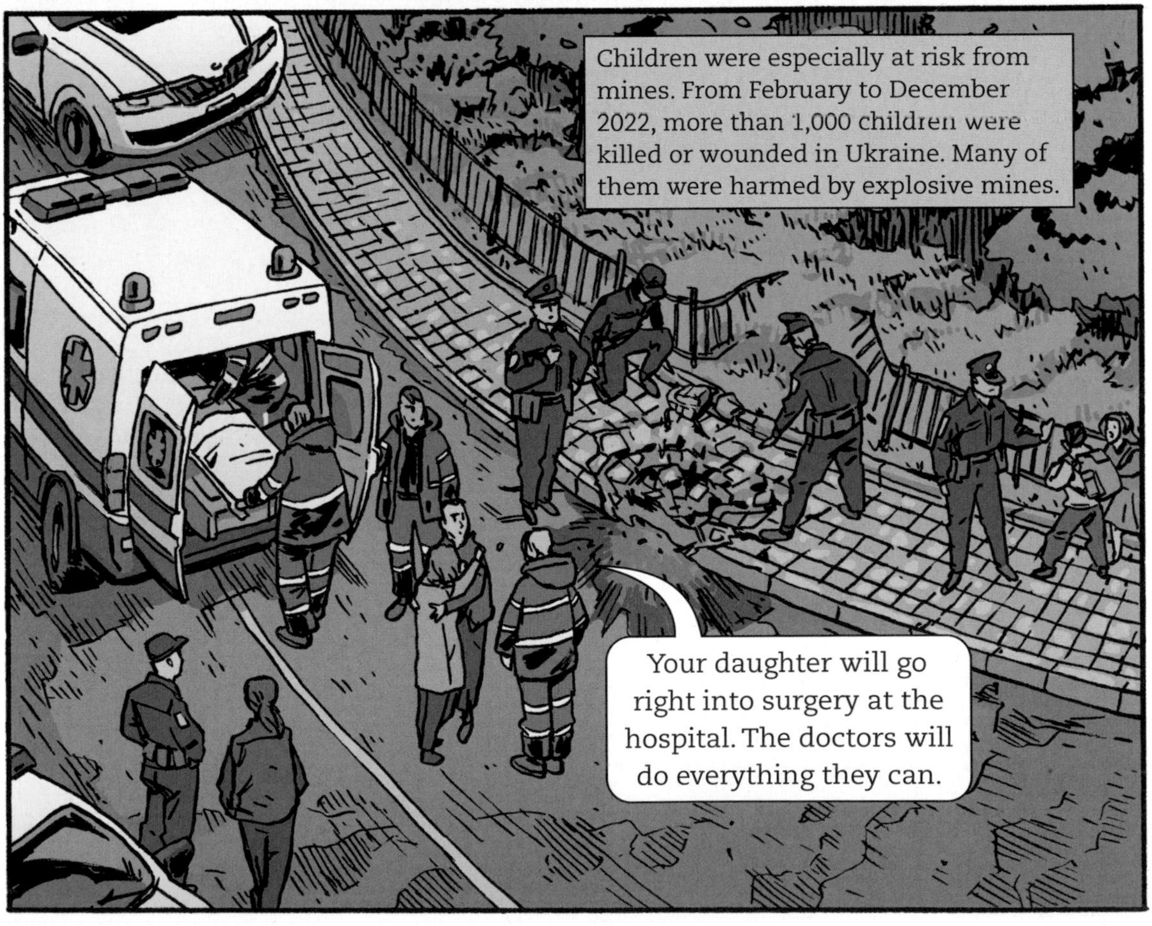
Children were especially at risk from mines. From February to December 2022, more than 1,000 children were killed or wounded in Ukraine. Many of them were harmed by explosive mines.
Your daughter will go right into surgery at the hospital. The doctors will do everything they can.

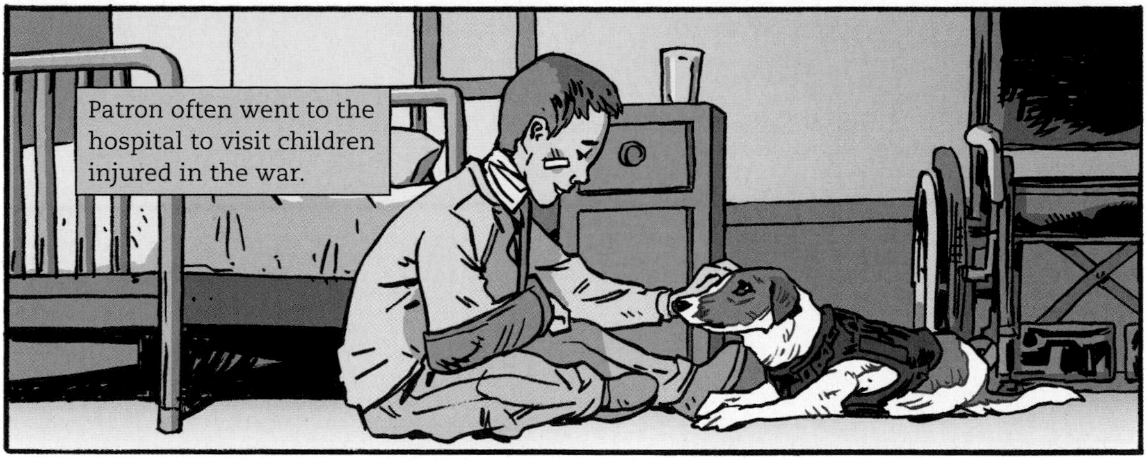
Patron often went to the hospital to visit children injured in the war.

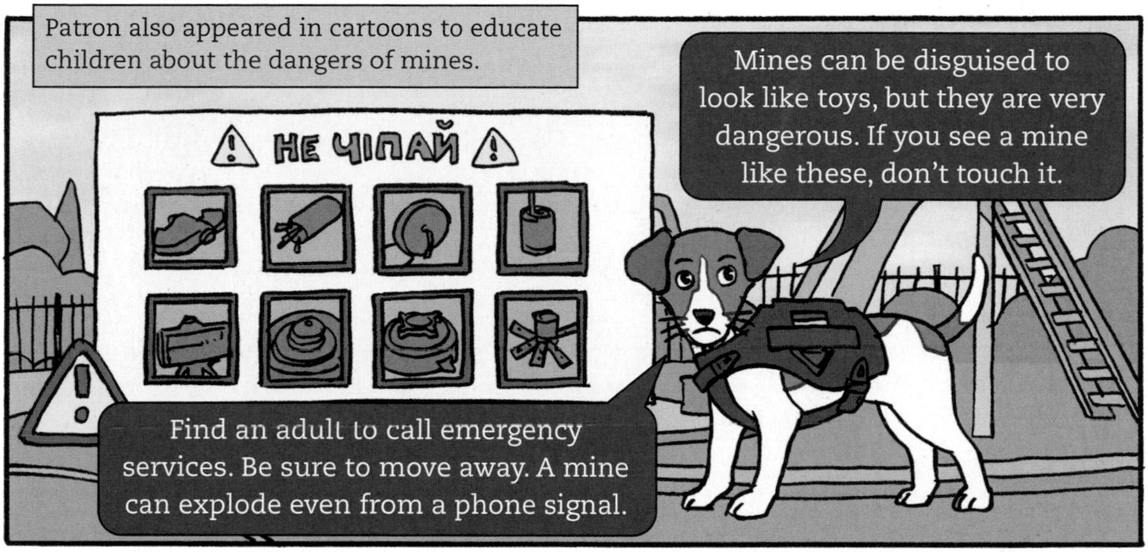
Patron also appeared in cartoons to educate children about the dangers of mines.
НЕ ЧІПАЙ
Mines can be disguised to look like toys, but they are very dangerous. If you see a mine like these, don't touch it.
Find an adult to call emergency services. Be sure to move away. A mine can explode even from a phone signal.

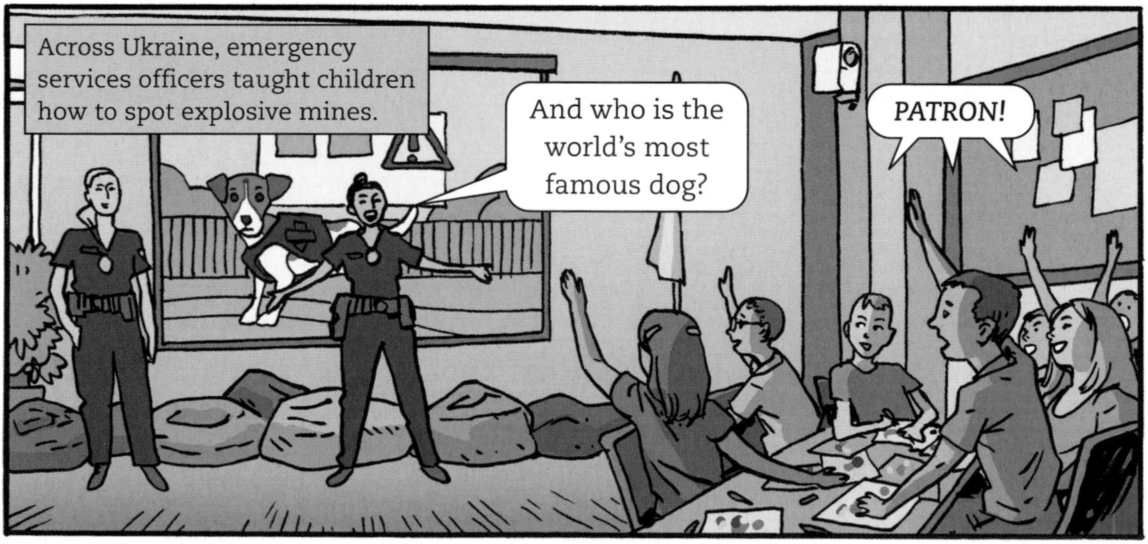
Across Ukraine, emergency services officers taught children how to spot explosive mines.
And who is the world's most famous dog?
PATRON!

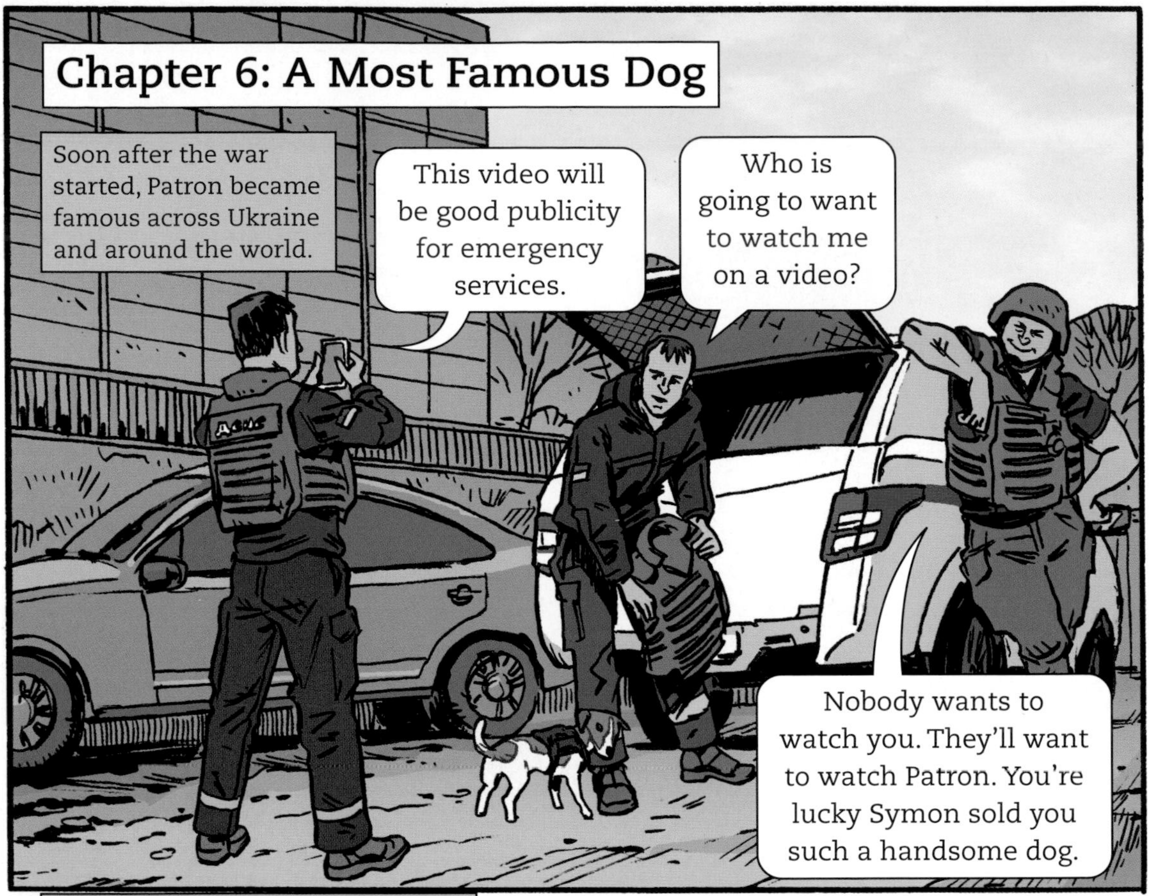
Chapter 6: A Most Famous Dog
Soon after the war started, Patron became famous across Ukraine and around the world.
This video will be good publicity for emergency services.
Who is going to want to watch me on a video?
Nobody wants to watch you. They'll want to watch Patron. You're lucky Symon sold you such a handsome dog.

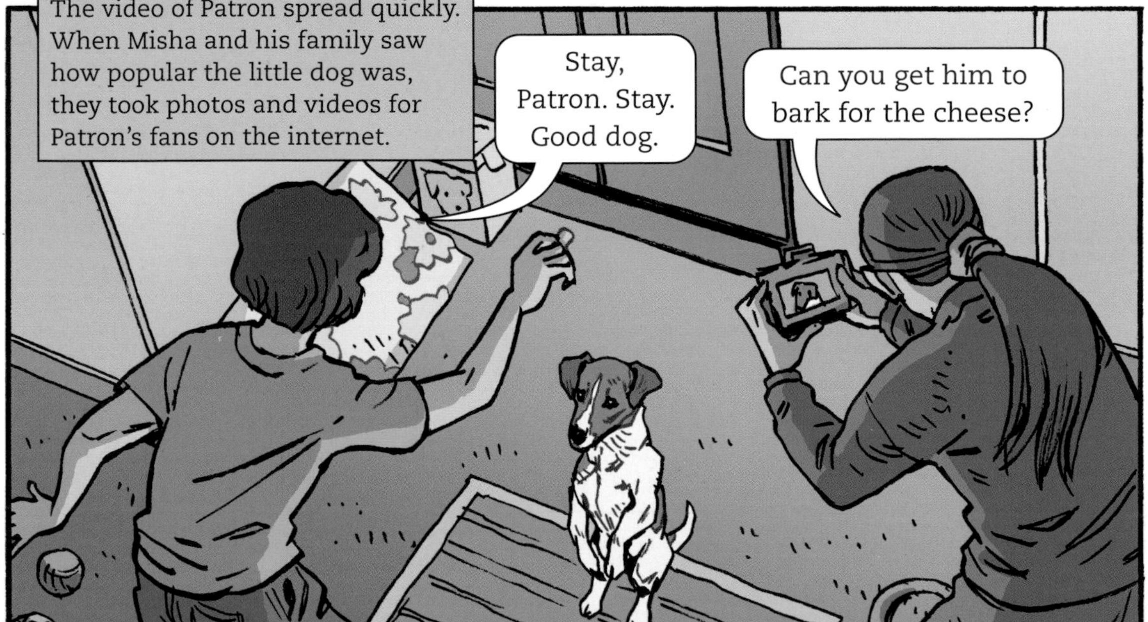
The video of Patron spread quickly. When Misha and his family saw how popular the little dog was, they took photos and videos for Patron's fans on the internet.
Stay, Patron. Stay. Good dog.
Can you get him to bark for the cheese?

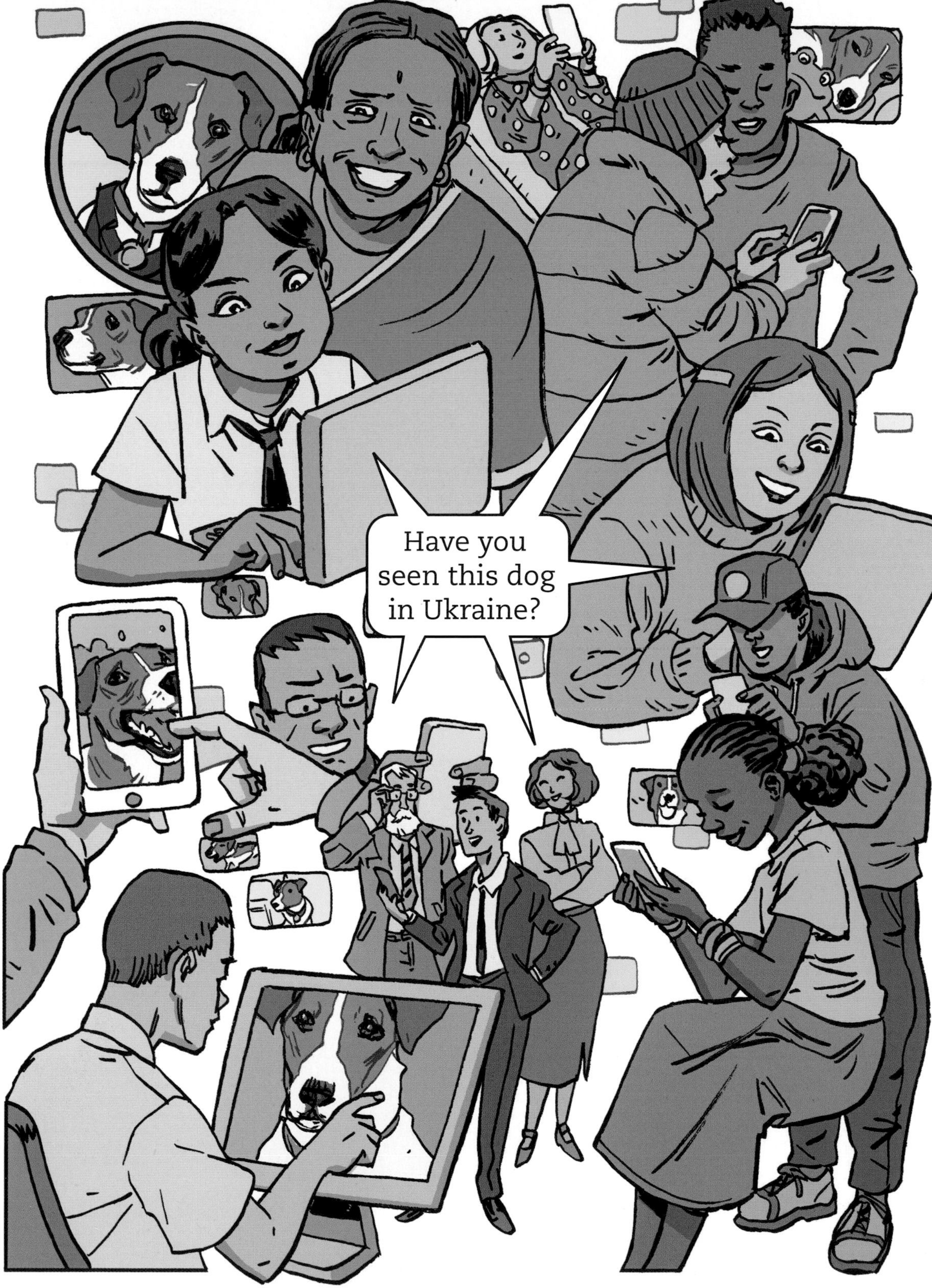
Have you seen this dog in Ukraine?

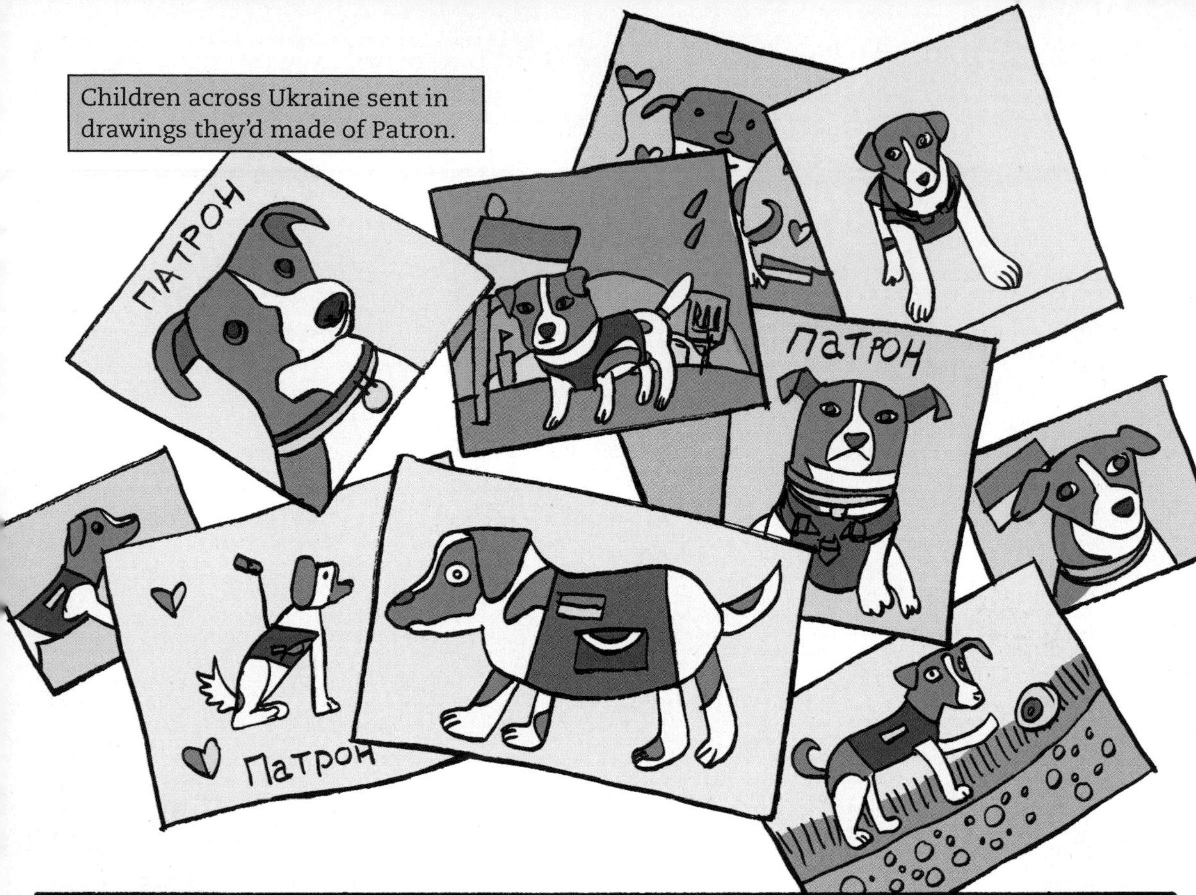
Children across Ukraine sent in drawings they'd made of Patron.
ПАТРОН
Патрон
Патрон

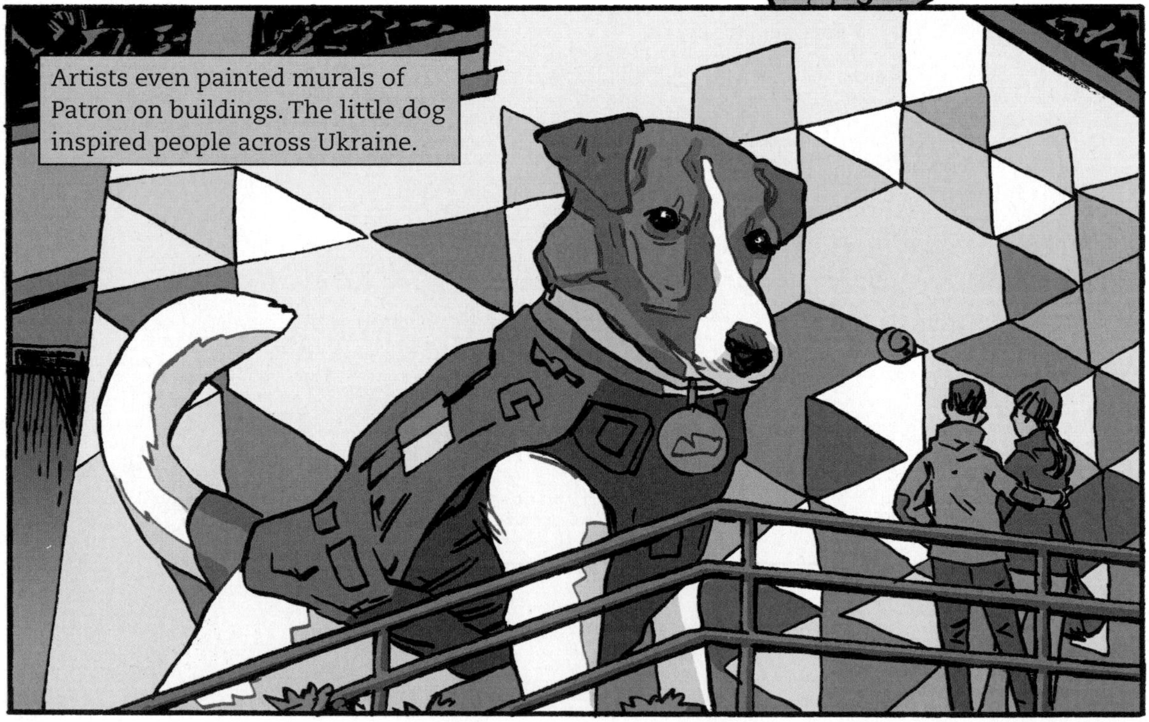
Artists even painted murals of Patron on buildings. The little dog inspired people across Ukraine.

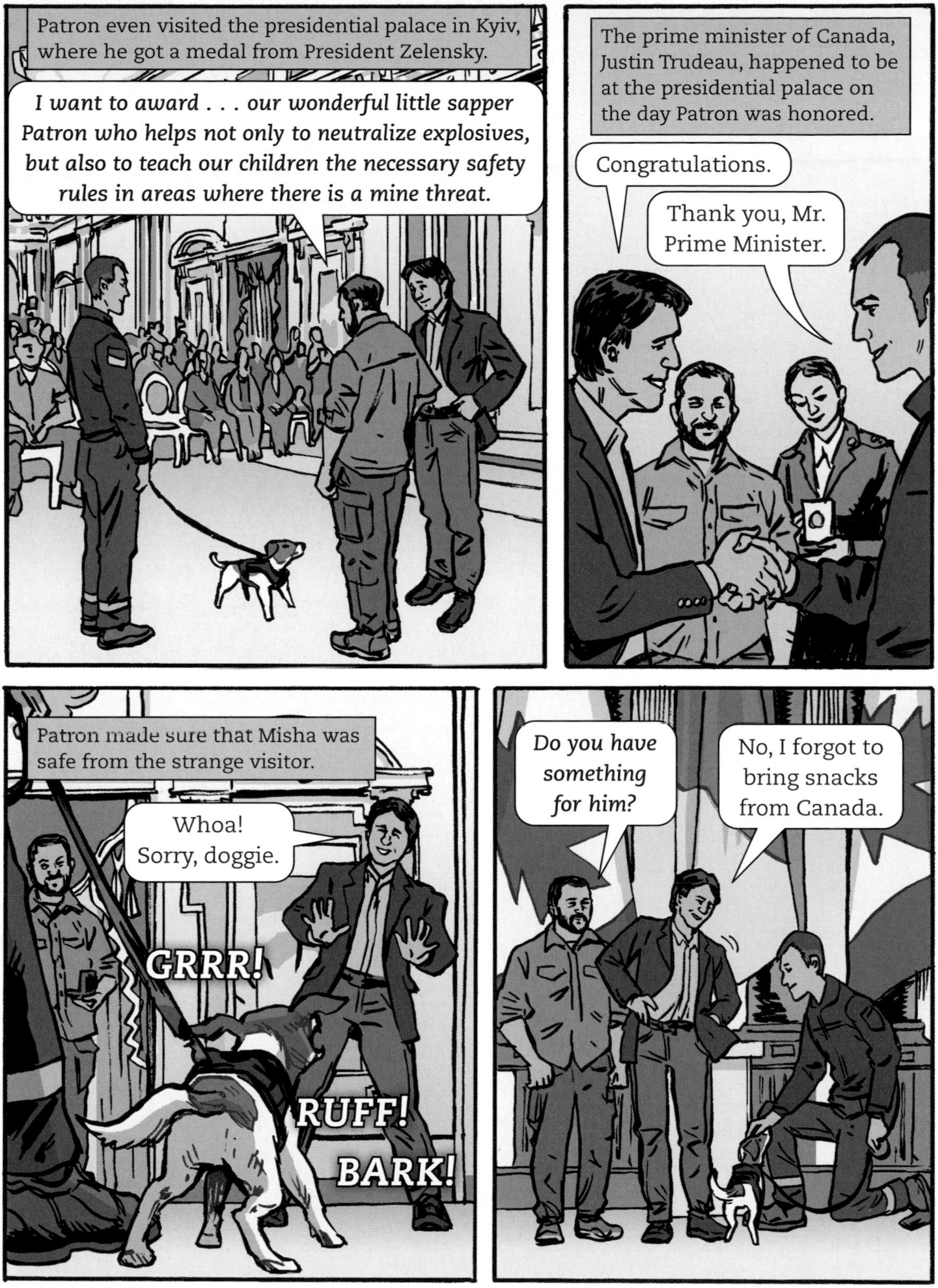
Patron even visited the presidential palace in Kyiv, where he got a medal from President Zelensky.
I want to award . . . our wonderful little sapper Patron who helps not only to neutralize explosives, but also to teach our children the necessary safety rules in areas where there is a mine threat.
The prime minister of Canada, Justin Trudeau, happened to be at the presidential palace on the day Patron was honored.
Congratulations.
Thank you, Mr. Prime Minister.
Patron made sure that Misha was safe from the strange visitor.
Whoa! Sorry, doggie.
GRRR!
RUFF!
BARK!
Do you have something for him?
No, I forgot to bring snacks from Canada.

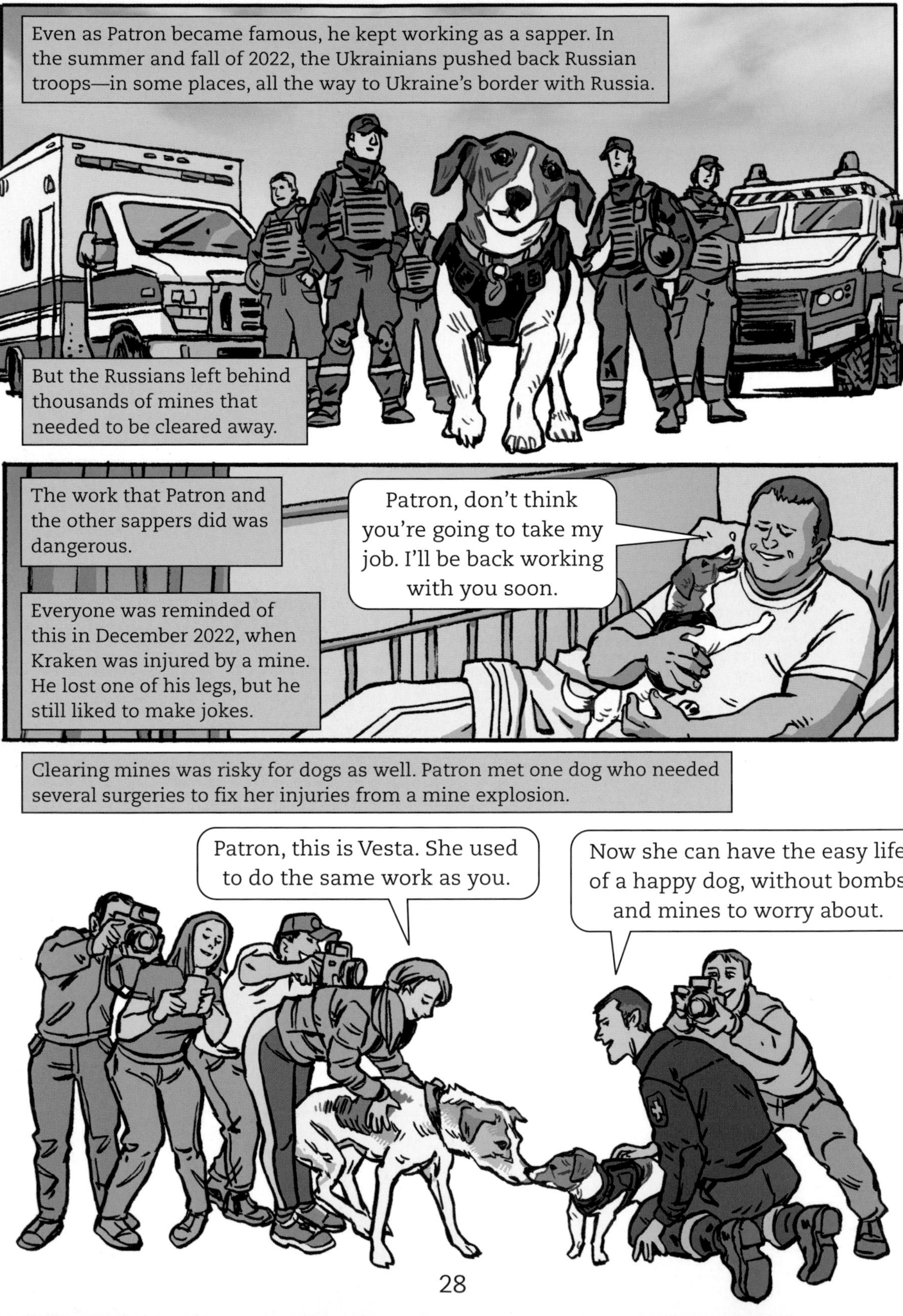
Even as Patron became famous, he kept working as a sapper. In the summer and fall of 2022, the Ukrainians pushed back Russian troops—in some places, all the way to Ukraine's border with Russia.
But the Russians left behind thousands of mines that needed to be cleared away.
The work that Patron and the other sappers did was dangerous.
Everyone was reminded of this in December 2022, when Kraken was injured by a mine. He lost one of his legs, but he still liked to make jokes.
Patron, don't think you're going to take my job. I'll be back working with you soon.
Clearing mines was risky for dogs as well. Patron met one dog who needed several surgeries to fix her injuries from a mine explosion.
Patron, this is Vesta. She used to do the same work as you.
Now she can have the easy life of a happy dog, without bombs and mines to worry about.

Ukraine's Smallest Hero

Patron was born in 2019. He is a Jack Russell terrier. Patron's owner, Mykhailo Iliev, is a major in the Ukrainian state emergency services. Patron began serving with the emergency services when he was only six months old.

In the first months after Russia invaded Ukraine in 2022, Patron helped to find hundreds of mines, bombs, and other explosive devices in the area around Chernihiv.

Patron first became famous on Facebook in March 2022. He soon had hundreds of thousands of followers on Instagram and TikTok.

Patron has received many awards, including a medal from Ukrainian president Volodymyr Zelensky. Patron has even been depicted on postage stamps in Ukraine.

In November 2022, Patron became the first dog ever to be named a "Dog of Goodwill" by the United Nations Children's Fund (UNICEF).

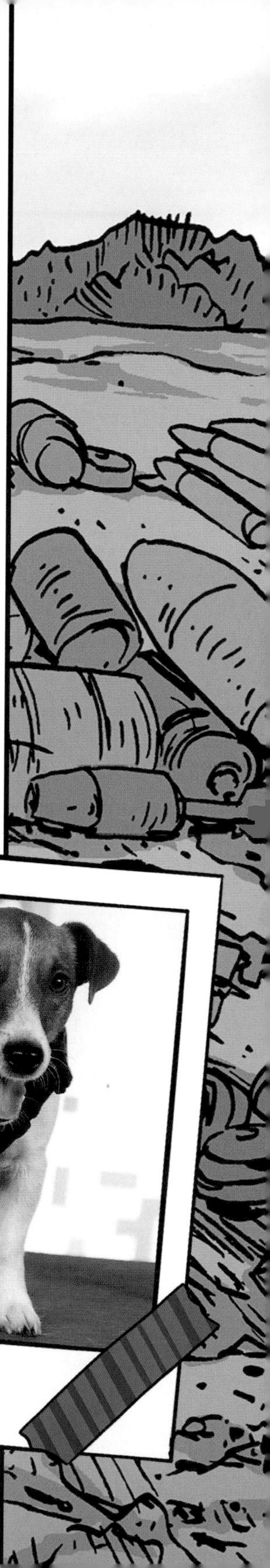

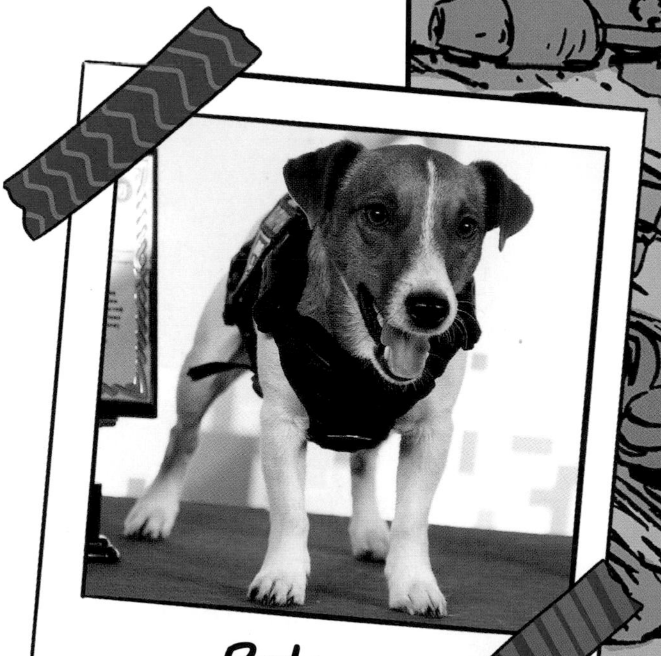
Patron

Glossary

artillery (ar-TI-luhr-ee) cannons and other large guns that fire shells at enemy forces from a distance

checkpoint (CHEK-point) a spot on a road or border where travelers are stopped for inspection

defuse (dee-FYOOZ) to remove the fuse from a bomb or mine so it won't explode

dispose (dih-SPOHZ) to remove and get rid of something that is harmful, such as a bomb or mine

invade (in-VADE) to send armed forces into another country to take it over

mural (MYOO-ruhl) a painting on a wall

pedigree (PED-uh-gree) a list or record of an animal's ancestors

purebred (PYOOR-bred) an animal whose ancestors come from the same breed

retreat (rih-TREET) to move back or withdraw from a conflict

spirited (SPIHR-ih-tuhd) having or showing courage and liveliness

surrender (suh-REN-duhr) to give up or admit defeat

technician (tek-NISH-uhn) a person who is skilled in working with tools and equipment

tenacious (tuh-NEY-shuhs) to be persistent or determined to achieve something

Read More

Berglund, Bruce. *Togo Takes the Lead: Heroic Sled Dog of the Alaska Serum Run*. North Mankato, MN: Capstone, 2023.

Jones, Trevor. *Major: A Soldier Dog*. Chambersburg, PA: Six Foot Press, 2019.

Lushchevska, Oksana. *Blue Skies and Golden Fields: Celebrating Ukraine*. North Mankato, MN: Capstone, 2023.

Internet Sites

News for Kids: Patron, Ukraine's Bomb-Sniffing Dog, Wins Award newsforkids.net/articles/2022/05/12/patron-ukraines-bomb-sniffing-dog-wins-award/

Patron the Bomb-Sniffing Dog Cements His Hero Status npr.org/2022/05/09/1097585032/patron-dog-ukraine-zelenskyy-medal

Patron the Mine-Sniffing Dog is Capturing Ukraine's Hearts today.com/parents/parents/patron-mine-sniffing-dog-capturing-ukraines-hearts-rcna25853

About the Author

Bruce Berglund was a history professor for 19 years. He has traveled to many countries to research history books, and has written about Eastern Europe, Ukraine, and Russia. He has had dogs as pets for his whole life. Bruce lives in Minnesota.

About the Illustrator

Mark Simmons is a freelance illustrator and cartoonist based in San Francisco. His past work includes comics for publishers such as Capstone, Behrman House, and Rebellion, as well as animation and advertising storyboards, animated operas, and other strange things. He also teaches comic art, figure drawing, and wildlife illustration for local zoos, schools, and museums. He loves animals of all kinds, especially bugs! For more info, visit www.ultimatemark.com.